EUROPA ✛ MILITAI
SPECIAL Nº2

THE
ROMAN LEGIONS
RECREATED IN
COLOUR PHOTOGRAPHS

DANIEL PETERSON

Windrow & Greene

© 1992 Daniel Peterson

Printed In Singapore by Craft Print Pte. Ltd.

This edition is published in Great Britain by
Windrow & Greene Ltd.
5 Gerrard Street
London W1V 7LJ

Reprinted 1996

A CIP catalogue record for this book is available from the
British Library.

ISBN 1-872004-06-7

Acknowledgements

The author wishes to thank the following
groups and individuals whose contributions
have helped make this book possible:
Legio VI Victrix (Roman Cohort Opladen)
for the use of photographs of the unit and
its reconstructions.
Legio X Gemina (Gemina Project) for the
use of photographs of the unit and its
reconstructions.
Legio XIIII Gemina Martia Victrix, and
especially unit co-founder, armourer and
'Optio' Steve Greeley.
*Legio XX Valeria Victrix (Ermine Street
Guard)* for the use of photographs of the
unit and its reconstructions.
Milites Litoris Saxoni for providing photo-
graphs at short notice of their 4th and 5th
century AD reconstructions.
Photographers: Fred Bauer, John Eagle,
Judy MacNamara and C.A.T. Media
Productions for the photos of *Legio XXI
Rapax and Ala II Flavia.*
Roman armourers: Michael Simkins, Chris
Dobson, Nigel Clough, Holger Ratsdorf,
Werner Bodensteiner, Steve Rogers, Len
Morgen, Tony Feldon and Ralf Eltner
(Leg XIIII catapult), whose reconstructions
appear, as well as the many talented
members of all the above reconstruction
groups who made much of their own
equipment.
Dr. Marcus Junkelmann for the use of his
reconstructions, photographs, horses, and
the opportunity to be a participant in his
several Roman cavalry experiments.
Dr. Dietwulf Baatz for the use of his
Sallburg on various occasions, as well as
information the Cremona catapult and
ancient artillery in general.
Susan Matheson and John Salomone for
details on the Dura Europos artifacts at
Yale University.

The EUROPA-MILITARIA SERIES

EUROPA-MILITARIA SPECIALS

BRINGING HISTORY TO LIFE

The accurate reconstruction and wearing of military costume of an earlier age is a tradition at least as old as ancient Rome itself. Just as the Beefeaters stand guard at the Tower of London in Tudor dress, or the Papal Guard in Renaissance costume at the Vatican, so the Praetorian Guard of Imperial Rome, when not on field service, carried the early *scutum* shield used in the Roman Republic centuries before, and other elements of their ceremonial dress undoubtedly harked back to those earlier times.

Today this phenomenon extends far beyond traditional guards or theatrical costumery. Professional interpreters, particularly at historic battlefield and fort sites in the USA and Canada, give visitors a glimpse of soldiers from the past – not only by dressing the part, but firing muskets, performing drill, and very often 'acting' the imagined personality of some long-dead soldier.

The vast majority of today's military re-enactors are not paid interpreters, however, but hobbyists from all walks of life who share a common interest in military history. In recent years they have gathered in their thousands to commemorate the anniversaries of famous battles, most notably those of the Napoleonic period, the American Revolution, and the English and American Civil Wars. When their impressions are historically accurate, these re-enactors can do much to bring to life the periods they represent, not only for the audience but for themselves. Certainly, to re-enact an actual historic march, with the precise equipment carried over the same terrain, can give a historian far more insight into a particular campaign than could ever be gained at home in even the best-equipped study.

Nevertheless, the vast majority of these 'living historians' can contribute very little new to our actual knowledge of military history, other than enlightening spectators and enjoying some self-gratification during the 'time machine' weekends they create for themselves. The periods most of these individuals strive to duplicate are seperated from our own time by only a few centuries at most. Generally speaking, sample collections of original equipment and uniforms used during these times are preserved in museums. Diaries and wartime reminisences from these eras are numerous. Regulations still survive, and thousands of receipts, vouchers, and forms detailing exactly what clothing soldiers were issued, what food they ate and what duties they performed are preserved in archives. All in all, we have a very good idea of military activities from the past few hundred years without a great need for reconstruction and experiment – illuminating though such experiments can often prove for the individual re-enactor who manages to 'get inside the shoes' of his chosen historical subject.

Only when these reconstruction activities are directed to times far more distant do we see a true scientific value – to those periods from which soldiers' diaries, printed regulations, and a wealth of physical material simply do not survive. In this respect, the reconstruction of ancient military equipment and experiments with its actual use are making great inroads into our relative ignorance of warfare in the classical world. Experiments made in the last decade have sometimes rendered the dogma of centuries obsolete. The Trireme Trust has answered questions and given us entirely new perspectives on ancient warships and their capabilities. The long-distance marching experiments of Dr. Marcus Junkelmann's *Legio XXI Rapax* over the Alps, and similar feats by other Roman reconstruction groups, have given us a glimpse of the endurance of the Roman soldier and how he must have carried his equipment. Roman saddle reconstructions by Peter Connolly, Dr. Junkelmann and others, and their actual use in simulated campaign and combat conditions, are proving that the Roman cavalry could perform admirably all the requirements of the mounted arm long before the so called 'stirrup revolution' touted in so many history books; and this writer feels honoured to have played some small part in these experiments.

No other army has captured the imagination so firmly as that of Rome. No army in history can match both its 3

Legio XIIII GMV with march packs. These are based primarily on their depiction on Trajan's Column. After only brief experimentation, it becomes clear that they cannot be carried high above their heads as the Column shows, but rather against the back. Methods of carrying the shield are discussed in the text.

longevity and its professionalism. It is no wonder that throughout the ages innumerable would-be 'Caesars' have taken the Roman eagle, and other attributes of that great army, for their own. How ironic it is that until the last decades of the 20th century these imitators and admirers never really knew what Roman soldiers actually looked like. True, pioneers in the field like Lindenschmidt and Couissin, in the late 19th and early 20th centuries, showed the world reasonably accurate reconstructions of the Roman soldier based on archaeological finds and provincial tombstone reliefs. Unfortunately, however, their work seems to have been largely ignored, as attested by the bulk of Roman soldier illustrations, film and theatrical depictions drawn almost exclusively from inaccurate interpretation of famous monuments in Rome.

It was largely the work of the late H. Russell Robinson of the Royal Armouries, HM Tower of London, summarised in his monumental volume *The Armour of Imperial Rome* (1975), that ushered in this 'new' era in which the Roman soldier, his armour and equipment are being reappraised for a wide public. (NB: As is now conventional, this book, like most others, follows the classifications of e.g. cuirass and helmet types suggested by H.R. Robinson.) There are now numerous books which give us a glimpse of what the Roman soldier probably looked like, some using actual reconstructions, but largely through the medium of colourful artwork.

This small book is the first attempt to make a fairly comprehensive examination of the development of the Roman legionary solely through the employment of actual full-scale reconstructions. This volume lacks the space to discuss in detail all of the experiments conducted and conclusions drawn through the actual use of these reconstructions; but we hope it will nevertheless make a valuable, if necessarily modest contribution to the task of bringing the late, great Roman army back to life.

4

BASIC CHRONOLOGY
of the Roman Republic and early Principate

The Roman Republic

(753 BC	Traditional date of foundation of city of Rome.)
510 BC	King Tarquinius the Proud expelled; Republic established.
270 BC	Rome completes extension of power over Italian mainland.
265 BC	Outbreak of 1st Punic War, against expansionist Carthage, over control of Sicily.
241 BC	Rome victorious.
219 BC	Outbreak of 2nd Punic War with Carthage, in Spain.
218-204 BC	Brilliant campaigns in Italy by Carthaginian general Hannibal.
206 BC	Decisive Roman victory in Spain.
202 BC	Final Roman victory at Zama; Carthage sues for peace.
200-168 BC	Series of campaigns against Macedonia end with decisive Roman victory at Pydna.
154-133 BC	Rome finally victorious in Spain against Celt-Iberian tribes.
149-146 BC	3rd Punic War; Carthage utterly destroyed. Rome now controls most of Mediterranean basin – Italy, much of Greece, Spain and North Africa.
111-106 BC	Rome finally victorious in bitter Jugurthine War in North Africa, under leadership of Gaius Marius.
104-101 BC	Marius defeats invading Cimbri and Teutones; Roman influence extends into southern Gaul.
91-88 BC	'Social War' in Italy leads to extension of Roman citizenship to, effectively, all Italians.

During the period from later Jugurthine War on, Marius reforms Roman army. Most important change is from short-time conscripts from property-owning classes, to open recruitment from all citizens. Poorer classes enlist in numbers, leading to birth of professional standing army.

88-65 BC	Mithridatic Wars against King of Pontus (approx. modern NE Turkey) end in Roman victory. Further campaigns of general Pompeius bring Syria, Judaea under Roman influence.
58-51 BC	Roman armies under general Julius Caesar eventually win final victory in genocidal Gallic Wars, bringing much of modern France under Roman control.
54 BC	Disastrous defeat of Roman army under Crassus by Parthians at Carrhae.
49-45 BC	Rivalry between Pompeius and Caesar leads to wide-ranging civil war; Caesar defeats Pompeius at Pharsalus, 48 BC, and subsequently rules as dictator.
44 BC	Julius Caesar assassinated.
44-31 BC	Complex, intermittent civil wars end with defeat of Marcus Antonius at Actium by Octavianus, great-nephew and heir of Caesar.
27 BC	Octavianus takes titles of 'Augustus' and 'Princeps', and becomes in all but name first Emperor of Rome.

The Principate

26-19 BC	Campaigns in Spain.
24-16 BC	Series of wars on north-eastern frontiers by Augustus and his stepsons, the able generals Tiberius and Drusus; Roman control pushed east into Germany, and north over Danubian area.
20-13 BC	War against Parthians in Armenia. Final campaign in Alps.
13-7 BC	Campaigns in Germany, and in Illyria (approx. modern Albania, Jugoslavia).

.... *(Birth of Christ)* ·······················

1–4 AD	Further campaigns against Parthia.
4-6 AD	Campaigns in southern Germany.
6-9 AD	Roman control established over Syria, Judaea. Illyrian revolt crushed.
9 AD	Campaign towards river Elbe ends in disaster with massacre of general Varus and three legions *(XVII, XVIII, XIX)* in Teutoberg Forest. No further major attempts to advance German frontier; north-east border of empire established roughly on Rhine and Danube, with limited buffer zone beyond.
14 AD	Augustus dies, succeeded on throne by Tiberius. By this date army more or less stabilised at around 30 legions plus rather larger and fluid force of auxiliary infantry and cavalry cohorts. Selective amalgamations lead to duplication of some legion numbers; but each legion now a permanent numbered, named formation, with long-term bases strategically placed inside imperial borders. Reforms of pay and conditions make army an attractive career; legionaries are regular long-service volunteers, increasingly recruited in European provinces.
14-18 AD	Mutiny in Rhine and Danube legions put down. Raids into Germany.
34-37 AD	War with Parthians in Armenia.
37 AD	Tiberius dies, succeeded by insane Gaius 'Caligula' Caesar.
41 AD	Caligula assassinated, succeeded by Claudius.
43 AD	Invasion of Britain commanded by Aulus Plautius.
54 AD	Claudius dies (assassinated?), succeeded by stepson Nero.
56-63 AD	Campaigns in Armenia and Mesopotamia against Parthians; general Corbulo achieves several victories.
60-61 AD	Major campaigns in Britain by Suetonius

	Paulinus; damaging revolt led by Boudica, queen of Iceni tribe in East Anglia, eventually crushed after heavy losses.
67-69 AD	General Vespasianus sent to put down Jewish revolt.
68 AD	Nero commits suicide in face of revolt led by Galba.
69 AD	'Year of the Three Emperors': Galba supplanted by Otho, and Otho by Vitellius. Eastern legions declare for Vespasianus, whose supporters defeat Vitellius at Cremona. Vespasianus ascends throne, establishes Flavian dynasty. (Nero's death ends final tenuous family connection with Caesarian dynasty, but name retained by emperors as honorific.)
69-71 AD	Mutiny on German frontier put down.
70-73 AD	Vespasianus' son Titus leads army in Judaea, captures Jerusalem; troops under general Silva besiege Masada, whose Jewish rebel defenders commit suicide on eve of fall of fortress in 73.
72 AD	Active conquest of Wales and northern Britain resumed.
79 AD	Vespasianus dies, suceeded by Titus.
81 AD	Titus dies young, succeeded by brother Domitianus.
83 AD	War against Chatti tribe in Germany; construction of *limes* (line of fortification in gap between Rhine and upper Danube) is begun.
84 AD	Victory of general Agricola in Scotland virtually ends initial offensive phase of conquest of Britain; fortresses established at Newstead and Oakwood.
85 AD	Dacian attacks repulsed in Moesia (approx. modern Bulgaria).
86-89 AD	Ultimately unsuccessful campaigns in approx. modern Hungary against Dacians, Marcommani and Quadi tribes.
89 AD	Mutiny put down on northern German frontier.
96 AD	Domitianus' assassination ends Flavian dynasty; he is succeeded briefly by Nerva.
97-98 AD	Campaigns against Suebi tribe on northeast frontier.
98 AD	Nerva dies, succeeded by adopted son Trajanus, an able soldier and administrator.
101-107 AD	Trajanus finally victorious in two hard-fought wars with Dacians in approx. modern Romania. Rome annexes modern Jordan.
c.105 AD	Roman defences north of Tyne-Solway line in northern Britain abandoned.
113-117 AD	Trajanus campaigns in Armenia and Mesopotamia against Parthians.
115-117 AD	Widespread Jewish revolts throughout N. Africa and Middle East are crushed.
117 AD	Trajanus dies, leaving empire at its greatest extent. He is succeeded by his nephew Hadrianus, who travels tirelessly around empire consolidating frontiers.
c.122 AD	After trouble in northern Britain Hadrianus supervises start of major defensive fortifications across Tyne-Solway line from North Sea to Irish Sea: 'Hadrian's Wall'.

132-135 AD	Bar Kochba's Revolt: self-proclaimed Messiah leads major Jewish rising in Judaea, harshly suppressed.
138 AD	Hadrianus dies, succeeded by adopted son Antoninus Pius.
c.143 AD	Revolt in northern Britain put down; frontier defences advanced to Forth-Clyde line, but this 'Antonine Wall' partly abandoned c.155, and finally in c.161.
161 AD	Antoninus dies, succeeded by nephew Marcus Aurelius. A philosopher and visionary, he is harried throughout his reign by constant frontier incursions, to which the armies respond with relative success although ravaged by epidemic plague.
162-165 AD	Campaigns against Parthians, ultimately successful, but returning troops spread plague.
166-175 AD	Series of major campaigns against Germanic tribes, Quadi, Marcomanni, Sarmatae; in 168-170 tribes cross Danube into Roman provinces, enter Italy, and reach Verona before being repulsed.
175 AD	Revolt in Syria put down.
178-180 AD	Further campaigns on Danube frontier.
180 AD	Marcus Aurelius dies, succeeded by unstable son Commodus.
180-184 AD	War in northern Britain; forts on Hadrian's Wall lost; general Ulpius Marcellus eventually restores order.
192 AD	Commodus assassinated, leading to widespread and damaging civil wars, 193-197, from which Septimius Severus emerges as victor. Incursions and risings on both northern and eastern frontiers.
195-202 AD	Campaign against Parthians in Mesopotamia.
208-211 AD	Severus and sons Caracalla and Geta campaign in Britain; major offensive into Scotland establishes order for many years, but permanent frontier remains Hadrian's Wall.
211 AD	Severus dies, succeeded by sons as joint rulers.
212 AD	Roman citizenship granted to all free born subjects within the empire, easing manpower recruitment for legions. Caracalla arranges his brother's murder and rules as sole emperor.
217 AD	Death of Caracalla heralds start of about 75 years of anarchy. Between Caracalla's death and succession of Diocletianus in 284 AD there are approximately 20 at least nominal 'emperors', of which only one is known to have died a natural death (from plague). Constant bids for power, either imperial or regional, by provincial generals and governors lead to endless civil war, the stripping of frontier garrisons with consequent incursions, etc. During 3rd century appearance and organisation of Roman legions are hardly known; archaeological record from military revival under able Balkan soldier-emperors of 4th century reveals a style of equipment unlike that of the 'classic' legionary.

THE LEGIONARIES

The origins of a true 'Roman' army seem to lie in the 6th century BC when Servius Tullius reorganized the federation of Etruscans, Romans, and Latins into a unified body whose troop types were classified by wealth rather than, as previously, by tribal origins. He divided the population into five property classes, the richest 'first class' being armed in the fashion of the Greek hoplite. This equipment consisted of a bronze helmet, cuirass, and greaves, a sword, a spear, and the traditional large, round hoplite 'Argive' shield. The first battle line of the field army was made up of 40 hundred-man 'centuries' of these troops, which fought in a Greek phalanx formation. The 'second class' troops were equipped like the first, except that they had no cuirass and used the native Latin *scutum* instead of the Argive shield; ten centuries of these troops were positioned behind the first class phalanx. Behind these were ten 'third class' centuries armed like the second class except that they lacked greaves. The 'fourth class' had neither helmet nor sword, but in addition to *scutum* and spear carried a light throwing javelin. The poorest, or 'fifth class', of which there were 15 centuries, were equipped as slingers. This army also had 18 centuries of cavalry recruited from the wealthiest families.

The second great change to Roman army organisation occured in the 4th century BC and is sometimes attributed to the dictator-hero Camillus. By this time the Argive shield-equipped phalanx had disappeared and the legion was universally equipped with the Latin *scutum*. The legion (*legio,* which originally meant 'levy') was split into three lines and had a strength of about 5,000 men. Front rank skirmishers called *velites* carried light javelins. The first two battle lines, the *hastati* and *principes,* were probably equipped with the now famous *pilum.* The third line consisted of three categories of spearmen – *triarii, rorarii,* and *accensi* – which, if we add the *hastati* and *principes,* may reflect the original five classes of the Servian army. We do not know if the armour worn in this period was still based on the original five classes, though it is likely that the *rorarii* and *accensi* (the latter's name literally meaning 'reserves') were still the most poorly equipped. The most common body armour was probably a round or square bronze breast plate, and the most popular helmets were probably debased Italian versions of the Greek 'Attic' and 'Corinthian' helmets, or the native Italian 'pot' helmets. The typical sword would be the leaf-bladed Greek hoplite type, or the curve-bladed *kopis* (possibly of Italian origin).

By the 2nd century BC the 'post-Camillan' legion was further refined. It now numbered some 4,200 men with the elimination of the *accensi* and *rorarii.* About 40 of

Above: Forerunner to the Roman heavy infantry legionary, a first class warrior of the 'Etrusco-Servian' Roman field army of the 5th century BC, essentially equipped in the fashion of a Greek hoplite of the period. Eighty 100-man 'centuries' of these troops formed the front line of the army, fighting in the phalanx formation with a nine-foot spear. The Greek-type sword shown here was a secondary weapon for use if the spear was broken. The helmet is the classic Greek 'Corinthian' model, though many other contemporary Greek and Latin styles were worn. The 'muscle' cuirass was the longest-used piece of 'Roman' armour, in use through 1000 years of Latin history. Only the first class troops carried the Argive shield, the remaining classes carrying the Latin *scutum.*

the light skirmishers were attached to each maniple ('handful') of *hastati, principes,* and *triarii.* The maniples of the two former divisions numbered about l60 men each, armed with *pila,* while a maniple of *triarii* numbered only about 60. These, the oldest (and thus perhaps best equipped) men, were armed like their predecessors with a nine foot spear instead of the shorter *pilum,* and could form a formidable defensive 'pike' formation as a last resort if the *hastati* and *principes* were forced to retire. Together, these three maniples of six centuries formed a *cohort,* ten of which comprised the legion. In addition there were 320 cavalry divided equally into ten units called *turmae.*

Military operations against new foes brought changes to the legionaries' equipment during the 2nd century. The Greek or Italian-type swords were replaced by the famous short, cut-and-thrust sword from Spain, the *gladius hispanicus* (which probably first came into contact with the Romans during the lst Punic War). The Roman *pugio* or dagger had a similar Spanish origin. The most popular helmet by this date was the Celtic 'Montefortino' type, great numbers of which may have been captured at Telamon and other Roman victories over the Celts. Likewise, Celtic shirts of ring mail found their way into the hands of the wealthier legionaries, and, like the Montefortino helmets, were probably being manufactured by the Romans themselves by this time. The typical body armour was a bronze chest plate, some nine inches square. Wealthier legionaries could provide themselves with better armour, such as Gallic mail or scale armour. In the case of officers, molded bronze 'muscle' cuirasses would have seen use. *Hastati, principes* and *triarii* all wore at least one greave (on the leading, left leg). All three divisions carried the *scutum,* of hide-covered laminated wood about two Roman feet wide by four feet high. The *velites* carried a round shield three feet in diameter; their only armour was a helmet, sometimes draped with an animal pelt. In addition to up to seven light javelins, they also carried the sword.

At the end of the 2nd century BC Marius reformed the legion, eliminating the *velites* and *triarii* and equipping all legionaries with the *pilum,* the classic long-shanked offensive throwing spear which characterised the legionary for perhaps 350 years. Six centuries each of approximately 80 men formed each cohort, ten of which again comprised a legion, now numbering some 4,800 infantry. This was essentially the legion of Julius Caesar and the early Empire, with one major exception. Possibly in Caesar's time (mid-1st century BC), but certainly by the mid-lst century AD, the first cohort of the legion began to be made up of five double-strength centuries instead of the usual six regular centuries. The organic cavalry in the legion was reduced to about l20 men; so at full strength the legion would number nearly 6,000 men.

The troops who could not afford their own armour were now issued it by the state (to be deducted from their pay, of course); and cheap, obviously mass-produced

Right: Interior of the Argive shield commonly used in both Greece and Italy; such a shield would weigh between 5 and 6kg, depending on whether it was faced in hide or bronze. The interior rim could be rested on the shoulder while in the phalanx or on the march, alleviating some of its weight.

Below right: The *kopis* was an extremely popular sword in the Mediterranean world from the 6th to 3rd centuries BC; some attribute its origin to Spain, though the earliest examples have been found in Italy.

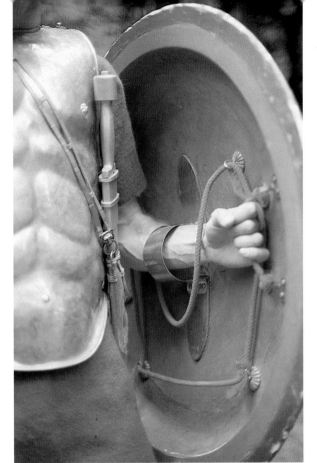

helmets begin appearing in this period. Mail or possibly scale shirt body defences were worn by all legionaries by this time. The Montefortino helmet was still the most common type, though Italian versions of Greek Attic and Corinthian helmets were also in use. Captured Gallic helmets of newer types, like the bronze 'Coolus' and iron 'Port' and 'Agen' types, were probably worn by legionaries in the mid-lst century BC, and as these areas fell under Roman control 'Romanised' versions of these practical helmets began to be manufactured for the army.

Above & left: Light infantry skirmisher of the Republican Roman army, based on the description by Polybius. Prior to the Marian-era reforms which abolished the various troop classes in the legion, 40 of these *velites* were attached to each maniple; they came from the lower class of citizens who could not afford the armour and equipment of the higher classes. His primary weapons are light throwing javelins, as many as seven sometimes being carried. By Polybius' time the famous *gladius hispanicus* would have been in common use, though this soldier still carries an old Greek-style sword. His shield was round, and three feet in diameter, made of wood or wicker and covered with hide. Here we show a spindle boss based on the bosses of contemporary *scuta* and round shields on the Aemilius Paullus monument at Delphi.

Opposite: Polybius stated that the *velites* sometimes wore pieces of animal skin on their helmets so that their centurions could judge from a distance how well they fought. This has been widely interpreted as wearing complete animal pelts, usually wolf skins as portrayed here, though this may not necessarily be the case. The wearing of animal pelts over the helmets by standard bearers during the Principate could, however, be a continuation of a tradition begun by the *velites* of the Republic.

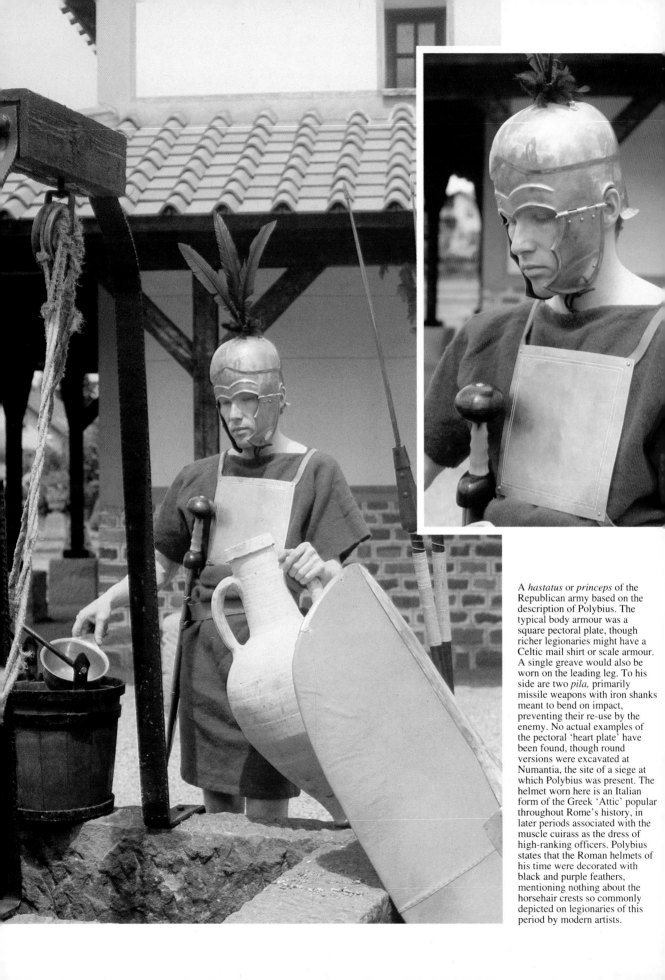

A *hastatus* or *princeps* of the Republican army based on the description of Polybius. The typical body armour was a square pectoral plate, though richer legionaries might have a Celtic mail shirt or scale armour. A single greave would also be worn on the leading leg. To his side are two *pila*, primarily missile weapons with iron shanks meant to bend on impact, preventing their re-use by the enemy. No actual examples of the pectoral 'heart plate' have been found, though round versions were excavated at Numantia, the site of a siege at which Polybius was present. The helmet worn here is an Italian form of the Greek 'Attic' popular throughout Rome's history, in later periods associated with the muscle cuirass as the dress of high-ranking officers. Polybius states that the Roman helmets of his time were decorated with black and purple feathers, mentioning nothing about the horsehair crests so commonly depicted on legionaries of this period by modern artists.

Above: Reconstruction of a 'Montefortino B' helmet dating from the late 3rd to early 2nd century BC. Though it has an applied rather than integral crest knob, it was finely made; its cabled border and engraved crest knob probably indicate private ownership. The Montefortino helmet seems to be the most prevalent type of the Republican period and, like ring mail, was Celtic in origin.

Left: A legionary of the Punic Wars. A more affluent *hastatus* or *princeps* might wear a mail shirt instead of a pectoral plate, as depicted here. Ring mail clearly seems to have been a Celtic invention dating to at least as early as 300 BC. Both the Celts and Romans wore mail shirts cut in imitation of the Greek linen cuirass with its distinctive shoulder doublings.

Polybius described the *scutum* as four feet high, made of two layers of wood glued together, and as thick as a man's palm. It was first covered with canvas and then with calf skin, and was reinforced at top and bottom with iron. This reconstruction is based on this description and an original specimen found in Egypt, and weighs approximately 10kg. There is no evidence to indicate that the shields of this period were decorated; Polybius makes no mention of decoration, despite his detailed description of legionary equipment down to the colour of their plumes. This seems to be supported by sculptural evidence; e.g. the Aemilius Paullus monument shows sculpted decoration on the Macedonian shields to depict their painted design, while the Roman *scuta* are left plain. Note the *gladius hispanicus,* adopted by the beginning of the 2nd century BC.

13

With the reforms of Marius at the beginning of the lst century BC the class system was abolished and the legions were opened to all citizens. Those who could not afford armour were issued it by the state. The basic appearance of the 'typical' legionary changed little in 250 years with mail shirt, Montefortino helmet, *pilum,* short sword and *scutum,* though there were some changes by the last century BC. This figure could represent a legionary of Marius, Julius Caesar or Augustus. The three-feather plume described by Polybius has now been replaced by horsehair, red being a colour mentioned in contemporary Roman texts and depicted on murals e.g. that of the soldier in the Pompeiian magistrate's court scene. By the late lst century BC the austere, unadorned *scutum* was clearly decorated, as attested by sculptural evidence. The necessity of unit identification by shield motif may have been brought about by Romans fighting Romans during the recurrent civil wars of this period.

IMPERIAL LEGIONARIES

With the end of the civil wars which left Augustus as the undisputed ruler of the Roman world, the legionary began taking on a different appearance. Though the Montefortino was still by far the most common helmet, improved versions appeared with a larger neck guard and brow reinforcement. The 'Coolus' helmets of Gallic origin also took on these improvements, and the first iron Coolus and 'Imperial Gallic' helmets, obviously produced in Roman workshops, began to appear. The *scutum* of Augustan date was 'clipped' of its top and bottom, reducing its weight. This modification has often been attributed to Augustan-period campaigns in the forests of Germany; but in fact the 'clipped' *scutum* may have existed since the time of Marius, when legionaries were first required to carry their full equipment on the march (not discounting the mid-lst century BC Ahenobarbus frieze, which indicates that some legionaries still carried the full-size *scutum* at this time).

Perhaps the most dramatic change in the appearance of the Roman soldier up to this date was the introduction of the laminated plate cuirass, known today as *lorica segmentata*, at about the end of the first quarter of the lst century AD. It has been suggested that this armour may have been produced quickly to equip newly-raised legions to replace the three lost in the Teutoburg Forest disaster. This is probably unlikely when we remember that only a few decades earlier Augustus disbanded some 30 legions, meaning that tens of thousands of surplus mail shirts were probably gathering dust in various Imperial armouries across the Roman world. It is more likely that the laminated cuirass was invented as a superior replacement for mail by skilled Gallic armourers in the Rhineland workshops which also produced the excellent 'Imperial Gallic' helmets of the same period.

This armour has been suggested by some as specifically the cuirass of 'Western' legions, while those in the East wore *loricae* of mail or scale. This was partially substantiated by the depiction of scale- and mail-clad legionaries on the Adamklissi monument. However, a recent discovery in Israel (in which this writer participated) has proven that *loricae segmentatae* similar, if not identical to those found in the famous Corbridge horde were used by the 'Eastern' legions in 68 AD during the Jewish Revolt. This distribution of an armour type whose origins are probably western European to the far-flung corners of the Roman Empire suggests a more sophisticated and uniform system of equipment supply than is usually credited.

16 A simpler version of the laminated cuirass was found at

Opposite: During, or perhaps by the Augustan epoch, the legionary began to take on a different appearance. New patterns of helmets began to appear, inspired as before by Celtic influence. This figure represents a legionary of *Legio XIIII Gemina;* the Gemina (Twins) title referred to its origin in the amalgamation of two earlier legions when Augustus reformed the army after the war with Marcus Antonius. Sword and dagger were suspended from two seperate belts crossed 'cowboy'-fashion: this *cingulum militare* became a proud mark of the military man, who often paid for handsome plate decoration. From early in the 1st century AD it began to be worn with an elaborate studded strap apron protecting the groin. The figure wears a Coolus type 'E' helmet based on the original thought to have been found in the Thames and now in the British Museum. On the pack saddle are two other variants of Coolus helmet: an iron Coolus 'C' based on an original from Oberaden, Germany, and another type 'C' of bronze from Schaan, Lichtenstein.

Inset: Detail of the 'Mainz' pattern *gladius*, the typical sword of an Augustan era legionary. Several scabbards of this style were found in the Rhine river at Mainz, hence the name.

Below: The long-pointed Mainz sword unsheathed and compared with its contemporary, the 'Fulham' pattern (right) found in the river Thames in that part of London. Behind the swords is a 'cut-down' style *scutum,* which was certainly in use by Augustus' time; it retains the curved side form of the large Republican shield,with the top and bottom shorn off. Some attribute this modification to the need to traverse rough terrain during Augustus' German campaigns, but it could well date from earlier, although the full size shields were still in use. The shield emblem is actually that of *Legio XIIII Gemina,* copied from a shield of that legion depicted on a grave *stele* of Gnaeus Museus.

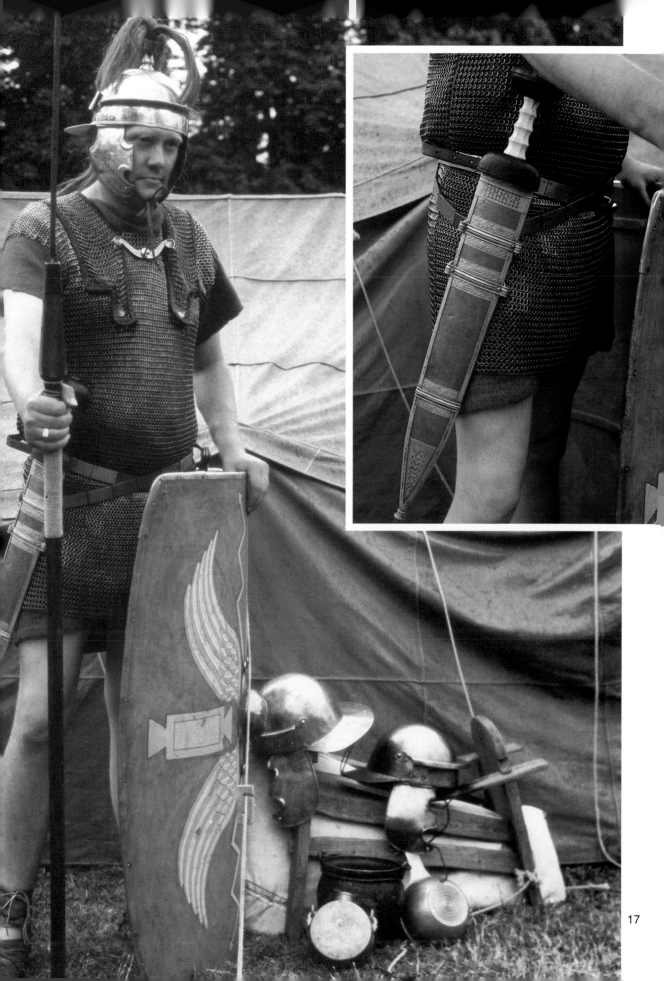

Opposite: Manning a rampart under a lowering northern sky, a member of *Legio XIIII* in the 'classic' legionary equipment of the mid- to late 1st century AD. He wears the Imperial Gallic 'D' helmet, the original of which was appropriately found in the Rhine at Mainz where *Legio XIIII* was stationed. The body armour is the Corbridge 'A' laminated cuirass, so named from the site in northern England where a chest containing a quantity of this type of armour was found. Probably manufactured in the Rhineland, this armour saw use throughout the Roman Empire; and this author first identified fragments of a shoulder unit while participating in the excavation of Gamala, a Jewish stronghold besieged by Vespasian in 67 AD. The *scutum* is shown in its final, rectangular form, its dimensions taken from a much later 3rd century example from Dura Europos, Syria. There is some evidence to indicate that elements of decoration, like the lightning bolts and cartouche or *tabula ansata,* may have been executed in light metal instead of paint: extensive use of metal decoration can be seen on the 1st century AD Doncaster shield (though this is thought to be auxiliary rather than legionary).

Left: The rear view of the legionary is rarely seen in sculpture or art. The upper chest of the Corbridge-type *lorica segmentata* is protected by single left and right plates; but the upper back is covered by three sets of overlapping lames. (Later sculptural representations seem to indicate similar lames on the chest.) The author has noted two major European museums in which this type of armour is displayed back to front through confusion over this point.

19

Newstead in Scotland and now seems to be dated to the end of the 2nd century AD. Legionary helmets of the 2nd century remained similar to those of the first, but are characterised by reinforcement bars across the skull, a feature thought to have been introduced during the Dacian Wars – possibly in response to the large,two-handed sickle-like sword used by these peoples.

By the 3rd century AD the laminated cuirass seems to have fallen into disuse, replaced by scale and mail shirts which now lacked the distinctive shoulder doublings of the earlier period. It seems clear that the laminated cuirasses of the lst and 2nd centuries never entirely superceded mail and scale armours, and it is likely that these different armours could have been used simultaneously in the same unit. Helmets became deeper, and with more pronounced sloping neck guards during the 3rd century; and the distinction between cavalry and infantry models may have disappeared. The longer *spatha* sword seems to have gained prominence in the infantry, though it still had not completely replaced the *gladius*. Swords, however, were by now always worn on the left hip rather than on the right as in earlier times, and suspended by a wide baldric.

The familiar tile-shaped *scutum* of the legions was still in use during the middle of the century, as evidenced by the finds at Dura Europos, Syria, but did not survive the century. The classic *pilum* seems to have given way to defensive thrusting spears and various javelins and 'darts'.

The 4th century Roman soldier presented a radical change from the vaguely similar types of the preceding three centuries. Most distinct was the adoption of a completely different helmet of western Asian origin, generally composed of a two-piece skull joined by a central ridge. These 'ridge helmets' were far cheaper and easier to manufacture than any previous form, and were probably the only practical solution to the problem

of arming the large new field armies of the period out of the severely depleted resources of the late Empire. The use of body armour in the infantry seems to have diminished, with the relatively greater importance of cavalry in the mobile armies, though some units were certainly still so equipped, principle types still being scale and mail. Some evidence suggests that molded rawhide cuirasses may also have been a common armour, though their appearance in period art may only reflect the persistent Roman tendency to 'Hellenise' armour, as in the case of the Greek Attic-like corruptions of Imperial Gallic or Italic helmets on Trajan's Column and other monuments. Shields were now universally round or oval,and very probably dished.

The *Notitia Dignitatum* of the very early 5th century indicates that some of the old 'legions' were still on the rolls, though by now their organisation would have changed considerably. Field army *legiones* numbered between 1,000 and 1,200 men, and no longer had integral artillery or cavalry. Exact organisation is unknown, though there seem to have been six 180 or 200 – man *ordines,* each divided into two *centuriae*.

The nature and character of the army had by now changed out of all recognition from that of the early Principate. Mobile field forces containing large numbers of semi-civilised mercenary allies manoeuvred across the Empire, fighting against constant barbarian incursions – and often, each other. Frontier garrisons were largely composed of locally recruited militia. By the fall of the Western Empire in c.410 AD a century and a half of rival generals stripping their provinces to pursue bids for the throne, and of administration dislocated by civil war, had destoyed the co-ordinated Empire-wide organisation which made the old regular legionary army such a marvellously impressive instrument.

The *lorica segmentata* can be taken off and put on by an unaided man, like a jacket, once the thongs linking the front fastenings of the girdle plates are untied; but it is quicker and easier if two comrades help one another. This also puts less stress on the straps, hinges and buckles, which are surprisingly fragile. The girdle and shoulder plates are held in flexible, overlapping articulation by being rivetted to internal straps; the girdle assembly and the chest, upper back and shoulder assembly are attached together by buckled straps in this Corbridge 'A' variant; Corbridge 'B' has them attached by hooks and loops – and also has seven, rather than eight, pairs of girdle plates. Archaeological finds indicate that type 'B' was already in use during the early stages of the Claudian invasion of Britain.

SWORDS AND DAGGERS

Opposite: In the early lst century AD a distinctly new form of sword began replacing the 'Mainz' style, little changed since its adoption from the Spanish. This new shape, with parallel-sided blade and short, clipped point, was christened the 'Pompeii' pattern after several examples of this type were found there. This *Legio XIIII* example is based on an original found at Mainz. Note the bronze 'Coolus' helmet on the legionary's chest; common sense quartermaster practice suggests that it would be unremarkable to see older pattern helmets in use with the laminated cuirass, though they are rarely combined in today's reconstructions or artwork.

Reconstruction of a Corbridge 'B' cuirass, with hook and loop fastening between girdle and chest plates. This ingenious armour weighs – depending on the thickness of the plates, which varies somewhat in archaeological finds – as little as 5.5kg. It consists, in the Corbridge 'A' type, of 40 seperate iron plates with bronze hinges and buckles; the 'B' type has 38 plates.

Below: A *Legio XX* Pompeii *gladius;* though this and the previous sword are basically the same, slight variations in design can be discerned. Roman military equipment was manufactured throughout the Empire, and though a basic uniformity in types of equipment can be seen, variations would be inevitable. It is important for modern reconstruction groups to present this accurate, 'uniform-but-different' appearance to the public.

Right top & bottom:
A comparison of two Pompeii *gladius* scabbard mounts belonging to *Legio X Gemina.* Below is another reconstruction of the 'Mainz' Pompeii *gladius,* and above is one based on mountings found at Oosterbeeck, Holland.

Opposite: An asssortment of decorated dagger *(pugio)* scabbards belonging to the *Legiones X, XIIII* and *XX* reconstruction groups, all based on original excavated specimens. As dagger scabbards and other equipment began to be excavated in numbers, their richness of decoration caused them to be classified at first as belonging to officers; but it is now clear that legionaries would also have possessed fine equipment. The highly decorative nature of much Roman equipment suggests that soldiers were proud of their appearance, being willing to invest considerable sums on decorated gear. (This may also have served as a practical way of carrying their 'wealth', though the Roman army did have an efficient banking system which allowed portions of salaries to be held for retirement or burial expenses.)

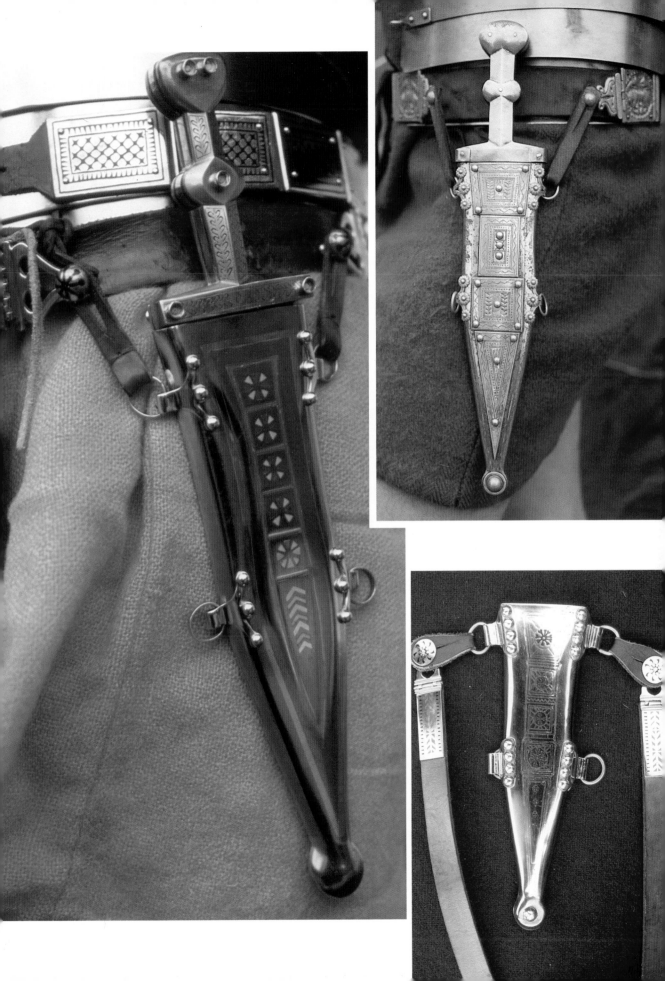

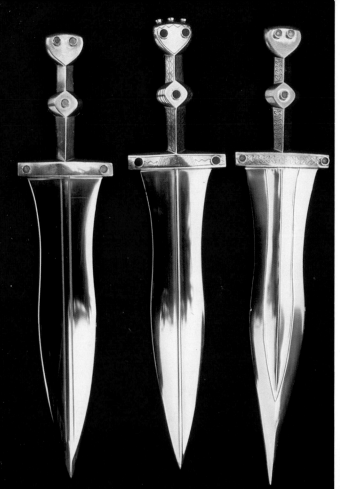

HELMETS

Opposite top: A collection of *Legio XIIII* helmets, all of which would have seen service in the mid- to late 1st century AD. *Top row,* left to right: bronze Coolus 'C' from Lichtenstein (on amphora), iron Imperial Gallic 'G' from Mainz, bronze Imperial Italic 'C' from Cremona, iron and brass Imperial Italic 'D' from Mainz. *Bottom row:* bronze Coolus 'E' from London, iron Imperial Gallic 'H' from Augsburg, bronze Imperial Gallic 'I' from Mainz.

Opposite bottom left & right: Another *Legio XIIII* reconstruction of a Mainz helmet lost in the Rhine, here an Imperial Italic 'D'. A very similar helmet was found in a rubbish pit at nearby Hofheim but had been stripped of its brass ornamentation. The eagle holding the laurel 'victory' wreath may have actual *Legio XIIII* associations: *Legio XIIII Gemina* left Mainz for the 43 AD invasion of Britain, returning in 70 AD having earned the additional title *'Martia Victrix'*.

Above: A good comparison of dagger blade variations belonging to *Legio XX*. Roman dagger blades were quite thin, and the ridges and grooves seen here increased their strength. The cast bronze handles would not be typical; most daggers had handles of thin, embossed sheet iron, making them surprisingly light.

Right: A richly niello-decorated double belt set belonging to *Legio XX*. The narrow plates and wide apron may indicate a belt more typical of Augustan or Tiberian date, though it could certainly have been worn with a laminated cuirass as seen here.

Above & right: Mid-1st century AD Imperial Gallic type 'G' helmet worn by a member of *Legio XIIII GMV;* this is the most popularly depicted version of the Imperial Gallic, though many reconstructions feature larger brow and neck guards. This example is copied exactly from the only intact original, found at Mainz and now exhibited at Worms.

Bottom of page: Another Mainz helmet from the Rhine, an Imperial Gallic 'G', but this time worn by *Legio XX Valeria Victrix* in Britain. While the only complete helmet of this type was found at Mainz, similar fragments were found in Colchester dating to the Boudican Revolt, making this the helmet of choice for *Legio XX.* Here, two examples are displayed with natural horsehair crests: virtually all Imperial Gallic and Italic helmets were designed to accept crests, which probably appeared similar to these reconstructions based on surviving crest supports and helmet attachment loops. Since no metal crest boxes have ever been found, they were almost certainly made of a perishable material like wood. These detachable crests may have fallen into disuse during Trajan's Dacian Wars when reinforcing crossbands began making an appearance. After this date no surviving legionary helmets show evidence of crest mounts, though crested infantry helmets are still depicted on monuments.

Opposite: Bronze Imperial Gallic helmets may have been more common than we imagine. Whereas iron helmets have been found in rubbish dumps, often stripped of their bronze fittings, the metal content of bronze helmets made them too valuable to simply discard. This Imperial Gallic 'I' worn by a *Legion XIIII* member is based on an original dredged from the Rhine at Mainz. Most Roman bronze helmets were found in similar circumstances, their accidental loss preventing their being 'recycled'.

29

Left & opposite: The most common helmet in the *Legio XIIII* reconstruction group is this Imperial Gallic 'H', with its characteristic deep skull and well sloped neck guard. The best original example is from Lech, near Augsburg. This was probably the 'typical' iron Imperial Gallic helmet of the later 1st century. Though the large, sloped neck guard is associated with this period, it is not reliable as a sole dating method. Early 1st century Imperial Gallic 'B' and 'C' finds – as well as an unclassified Augustan helmet from Haltern – all exhibit this feature; for as yet unexplained reasons the neck guards tended to become shorter and nearly horizontal for a period in the mid-century.

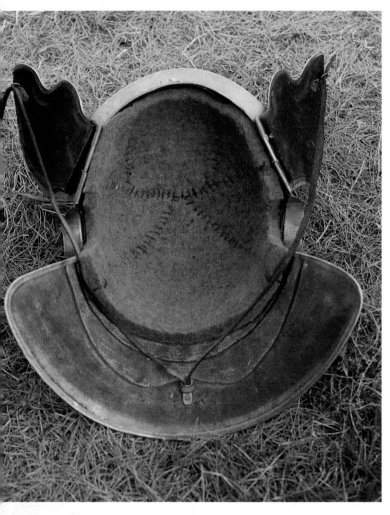

Above left & right:
Reconstruction of an Imperial
Italic type 'G', the original of
which is said to have been found
in a cave near Hebron, Israel, and
thought to date from the Bar
Kochba revolt in the early 130s
AD. The crossed reinforces are a
feature which seem to have
originated during Trajan's
Dacian Wars, perhaps a response
to the formidable Dacian *falx,* a
sickle-like two-handed sword.
The first sculptural evidence
comes from Trajan's Column
and the Adamklissi monument;
and an excavated Imperial Gallic
helmet from Romania, dated to
the Trajanic campaigns, has the
reinforces overlaying the
embossed skull decoration,
indicating retrospective
modification. The *luna* motif is
so positioned on this example as
to indicate that the cross-bracing
was a feature of its original
manufacture.

Left: Speculative reconstruction
of a helmet liner made of thick
felt. There is isolated
archaeological evidence for the
use of liners glued in place,
including a fragment of glued-in
felt on a find from Newstead,
Scotland, and linen lining on
cheek guards. Some form of liner
was obviously necessary, and
excavated helmets show no sign
of holes for attachment by
stitching or rivetting. Note also
the embossed strengthening ribs
in the neck guard; and the rings
for attaching the thong.

Opposite: see caption overleaf.

Opposite: During the relative 'dark age' of the anarchic 3rd century the long evolution in Roman helmet design, from early Celtic models through the impressive Imperial categories, apparently came to an end. The fragmentation of the Empire's military resources can presumably be blamed, as well as contact with the products of other peoples. When the archaeological record picks up again in the early 4th century we find this Romano-Sassanian 'ridge helmet', radically different from earlier equipment and probably copied from Sassanian Persian models. A fine example was found with the skeleton of its owner in a collapsed siege mine at Dura Europos; made in two parts joined by a central ridge, or in half a dozen panels in *spangenhelm* fashion, these helmets seem to have had cheek and neck guards attached only 'lining to lining' and by buckled straps respectively. The type at left is usually classed as 'infantry', the other as 'cavalry', based on the covered ears that differentiated earlier cavalry helmets. A better classification might be 'light' and 'heavy': infantry skirmishers and light horse may have worn the former, heavy infantry and cavalry the latter.

The Late Empire

Previous page: A legionary of the late 2nd or early 3rd century AD, as a hundred years of darkness began to fall over the Empire.... He wears the Auxiliary Cavalry 'E' helmet, which though classed as cavalry was probably also in use by the infantry of this time: a helmet of very similar form with enclosed ears is clearly depicted on the grave *stele* of Aurelius Suro of *Legio I Adiutrix* in the early 3rd century. The laminated cuirass is of the Newstead pattern – made of fewer, larger plates than the Corbridge type – and is probably Antonine in date. (Interestingly, fragments of the helmet were also found at Newstead and assigned this date.) His *scutum* is based on the example from Dura Europos, and dated to that city's fall to the Persians in the 3rd century. Though still in use, the *pilum* was beginning to be superceded by a thrusting spear. The *gladius* was being replaced by the longer *spatha,* worn here on a wide baldric as was becoming the fashion.

The Dura Europos *scutum,* much discussed, is held by some to be a 'parade' item, on the grounds of its elaborate paintwork and relatively thin construction. It is edged with leather (as are the oval shields from the same find), but bronze edging finds indicate that 1st and 2nd century battle shields were often no thicker. Elaborately painted battle shields were characteristic of earlier Mediterranean armies; and today we may place too high a 'rarity value' on skilled painting to appreciate its availability in the ancient world. A skilled slave could paint such a shield in two days, and as any given unit would see action relatively infrequently such a shield would give years of service before needing replacement.

Above & right: Details of the helmet, and Newstead cuirass. The claim that the latter was an improvement over the Corbridge type – in any sense other than greater simplicity of manufacture, and more robust fittings – would be disputed by anyone who has worn both types over any length of time. The Corbridge *lorica* is more comfortable, and offers a greater range of movement.

Left, above & opposite:
Reconstruction of a junior officer of infantry, early 4th century AD, by the *Milites Litoris Saxoni.* The legionary who emerges from the evidential mists of the 3rd century bears little resemblance to the classic *miles legionis,* last seen as the darkness closed over the army of Caracalla. The helmet is modelled on one of four found at Intercissa, Hungary, and the only one bearing the metal crest, which suggests junior rank. Of 'ridge' design, the silvered iron headpiece is decorated with non-Christian cross symbols, 'new moon' horns, and eyes. The leather edging, method of fastening the cheek guards, and buckled attachment of the neck guard are assumed.

The tunic with tapered sleeves *(strictata)* and appliqué decoration is from a junior officer figure in the Piazza Armerina mosaic in Sicily – the 'swastika' device shown on the skirt of the original has been omitted, to avoid wearisome argument with ill-informed members of the public.... The long trousers are found on *stelae* of the 2nd century and thereafter.

The long *spatha*-type sword, modelled on one of two found in the so-called 'murder grave' of two soldiers at Canterbury, is attached – by a speculative arrangment of strapping – to a broad baldric. The decorative fittings of the baldric are taken from several known examples (e.g. finds now at Carlisle, Vindolanda and Silchester); the pierced motto is *'Optime Maxime Con(serva) Numerum Omnium Militantium'* - '(Jupiter) Greatest and Best, Protect This Unit, Soldiers All'. The large scabbard chape in rondel form is typically 3rd century, and perhaps survived later.

The quartered shield with a boar motif is from the Piazza Armerina mosaic, its size and construction taken from the Dura Europos find; it has a single central grip and a pointed boss. The late spear, of *angon* type, is one of many styles excavated. (Reconstruction by John Eagle, worn by Robin Brenchley; photographs John Eagle)

Below: An alternative broad, 'bellied' spear type, after the 'Sewing Field' find; and a shield design from the early 5th century *Notitia Dignitatum,* identified as that of the *Britones Seniores,* a *legio palatina* then in Illyricum but formerly in Britain – perhaps the last descendants of the old *Legio XX Valeria Victrix?*

CENTURIONS

The rank of centurion seems always to have been an integral part of the Roman army, for the 'century' had been an element of troop organisation dating as far back as the Servian Etrusco-Roman field army. Originally the centurions were elected by those in their century; later, they seem to have been appointed by their *tribunes* (effectively, the legion's 'staff officers') with approval authority in the hands of the legion or army commander. During the Principate centurions were appointed by the governor of the province in which the legion was garrisoned, but this was probably on the recommendation of the legion commander or subordinate tribunes. Even the Emperor could intervene in the appointment of centurions should the prospective candidate have influential friends.

Centurions are often associated with modern non-commissioned and warrant officers, as they would often 'rise through the ranks', but this was only one way a centurionate could be obtained. Praetorians could be appointed legionary centurions following their mandatory 16 years of service in the Guard. Even *equites* (knights) could apply for 'direct commissions' to the rank of centurion from civil life. (If we equate a legion, solely on the basis of size, with a modern brigade, then we may say that all appointments from half-company up to battalion commands were filled by centurions of various grades of seniority – though such modern approximations should not be taken too far.)

The highest centurial rank was that of *primus pilus* – 'first spear' – the senior centurion of the First Century in the First Cohort. This rank was normally held for one year, after which he would retire or be appointed 'camp prefect', responsible for the legion's equipment and transport. These men could still go on to better things, as there are accounts of former 'first spears' commanding fleets, or the Praetorian Guard, or even becoming governors (of provinces in which only auxiliaries were garrisoned).

During the Principate the legion normally had 59 centurions, one for each of the five double-size centuries in the First Cohort, and 54 for the remaining normal-size centuries (nine cohorts each with six centuries). Each centurion had a staff of 'non-commissioned' officers to assist him in his duties: the *signifer* (standard bearer), who in addition served as the unit 'banker'; the *optio,* who would take over if the *centurio* fell, and who could be considered the 'training officer'; and the *tesserarius,* whose function would be similar to 'officer of the guard' or company senior clerk.

Opposite: A late Augustan *centurio* of *Legio XXI Rapax.* The Imperial Gallic 'C' helmet he wears would represent the very latest in design, and might well be in the hands of centurions alone by this early date. Some Roman authorities may feel the large Republican *scutum* to be somewhat anachronistic with this helmet, but as so often in this field, there is not enough evidence to be certain one way or the other.

Above: Tombstone of *centurio* Titus Calidus Severus, a mid-1st century AD officer; it shows his scale armour, greaves, helmet with *crista traversa,* and – of particular interest – his servant holding his horse. Some centurions clearly owned horses, certainly *primi ordines* of the legion's First Cohort, though they would normally be ridden on the march rather than in combat.

Opposite: The 'favourite' centurion impression that most modern reconstruction groups have attempted to duplicate is Marcus Favonius Facilis. Facilis' grave *stele* dates to the mid-1st century AD, which is the approximate period most reconstruction groups depict. The *centurio* of *Legio X Gemina* in the Netherlands poses here exactly as Facilis appears on his *stele*. The body armour is certainly mail, though the *lorica* is cut in a distinct and unusual form, seemingly in imitation of a molded cuirass; the extremely long shoulder doublings are also unique to this *stele*. As invariably seen on other centurions' grave *stelae*, the sword is worn on the left, the opposite side to that of the legionary. The omnipresent symbol of the centurion, his vine staff or *vitis*, is clearly depicted on the *stele*. Unfortunately no helmet is shown on the Facilis monument.

Right: The most appropriate group to reconstruct the costume portrayed on the Facilis *stele* is, of course, *Legio XX VV,* the actual unit of the deceased. Had Facilis lived longer he might have been awarded a fine set of *torques* and *phalerae* as worn here by his modern counterpart. While this set of decorations is not based exactly on any particular set depicted on a tombstone, it is representative of many 1st century AD examples. Based on the sculptural record, the most common number of *phalerae* which make up a set is nine, but sets of seven, five, and ten are also known. The helmet is the Imperial Gallic 'G', which corresponds well to the mid-1st century date of the Facilis *stele*.

Right: A detachment of *Legio XX* under command of centurion Facilis has just entered a turf and timber fort garrisoned by auxiliaries. The ramparts are of turf-faced earth, topped by a timber wall walk and crenellated pallisade, and the gatehouse is entirely of timber. These forts, typical of frontier posts usually held by single auxiliary cohorts, could eventually be rebuilt in stone if the line of defences became permanent; or could be burnt and levelled if they were abandoned. This example was built at The Lunt, Baginton, near Coventry, England, by men of the Royal Engineers, as an archaeological experiment to gauge the rate of deterioration of such defences. There is a reconstructed fort granary building as well as the gate and wall section; this now houses a museum.

Opposite: A final version of Facilis, this time reconstructed in Germany by *Legio VI Victrix*. Unlike the original, in which a single, wide, plated belt is worn, this *centurio* wears a set of double belts with ball terminals similar to the two found on a skeleton in Herculaeneum. His helmet is the bronze Imperial Gallic 'I'. During the Roman Republic the vast majority of helmets were bronze, so those of centurions were often tinned or silvered for smartness or recognition. (Perhaps in the Principate, when bright, silver-like iron helmets became commonplace, some centurions may have preferred bronze, to remain more conspicuous in the field?)

Opposite: As a departure from the rest, the *centurio* impression of *Legio XIIII Gemina Martia Victrix* is based on the *stele* of Q. Sertorius Festus, a centurion of *Legio XI Claudia Pia Fidelis,* also dated to the mid-lst century AD. The helmet used here is the Imperial Gallic 'H' from Augsburg with a feather, instead of horsehair, *crista traversa,* as clearly depicted on the *stele* of Marcus Petronius Classicus. Festus wears a set of seven *phalerae;* but instead of duplicating those (some of which are now illegible) on the original monument, the finest actual set occuring in archaeology were duplicated: these are the Lauersfort Phalerae, discovered in l858 near the site of the legionary fortress of Vetera in Germany. The *torques* on the Festus *stele* are nearly the same diameter as the *phalerae,* so may actually be *armilla* (bracelets) as represented here.

Regular scale armour is inferior to mail, raising the question why this seems to have been a preferred armour of many centurions in the sculptural record. The answer may be that some of the scale defences seen on the *stelae* are actually representations of the *lorica plumata,* scales 'ribbed' for extra strength and attached to a base of ring mail – as replicated in this reconstruction using nearly 8,000 individual scales. Such an armour would be a more attractive and effective defence than normal mail (albeit much heavier, as the author can confirm).

Above: A reconstructed wooden barracks block in the Saalburg fort near Bad Homburg, Germany. Rebuilt on the original location in the late 19th century, this is the most complete existing reconstruction of a Roman military site. This barrack would have housed a century of 80 legionaries and the living quarters and office of their centurion. Here a detail from *Legio XIIII* are addressed by their *centurio;* the soldier at the near end of the rank is the *optio,* the centurion's second-in-command.

STANDARDS

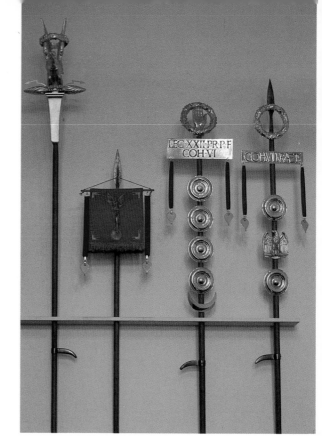

The best known of all Roman standards was the *aquila* (eagle), emblem of the legion. Prior to the reforms of Marius in the 2nd century BC, minotaurs, wolves, boars, and horses were also legionary standards, possibly denoting the different tribal origins from which the legions were recruited.

In addition to the *aquila* legions carried secondary standards. The best authenticated examples are those related to the signs of the Zodiac, indicating the particular legion's 'birth month'. It has been attractive for modern writers to assign distinctive non-zodiacal symbols to those legions whose birth month is unknown, but with which some other symbol may be associated. This individuality in legion emblems fits well into our modern concepts of distinctive unit insignia; but unfortunately has yet to be substantiated in the Roman army, except perhaps in the matter of shield decoration. For example, some of these hypothetical legion emblems are based on a single stamping in a clay tile. The theory suffers in cases where a number of different emblems have been identified on tiles or *stelae* of the same legion. For some legions, such as *Legio XX Valeria Victrix*, there is fairly good evidence for the use of a non-zodiacal legion symbol, in this case a wild boar. Perhaps those legions 'born' in a month which lacked an appealing symbol could adopt a different one? The boar was certainly used as a military emblem under the Roman Republic.

During the Principate the portrait of the emperor (*imago*) also seems to have been carried by each legion. The grave *stele* of Genialis of the *Cohors VII Raetorum* shows that auxiliary cohorts also possessed the *imago*, perhaps indicating that each legionary cohort may also have carried this standard.

For detachments operating away from the main unit, at least in the case of legions, a horizontally-hung cloth flag known as the *vexillum* was carried. It has been popular in modern reconstruction to show the various legion emblems painted or embroidered on these flags. Most examples in Roman sculpture are now devoid of design (emblems or inscriptions being applied in paint and long since vanished); though there are some exceptions, all of which show lettering alone. For example, an inscribed *vexillum* depicted on a stone tablet from Benwell on Hadrian's wall reads: '*LEG II*'. Flanking this *vexillum* on the tablet, though not depicted on the *vexillium* itself, are the Capricorn, denoting the legion's birth month, and a Pegasus, probably a secondary legion emblem. A second tablet, commemorating construction of a length of the Antonine Wall, depicts another Second Legion *vexillum*, also devoid of symbols except for the inscription '*LEG II AUG*'.

cohorts probably carried the *signum*. While there are seemingly endless small variations to these as depicted in Roman sculpture, they are basically an assemblage of discs (*phalerae*) mounted on a pole surmounted by a spear point or effigy hand. These variations probably date to the manipular legion of the Republic, the hand (*manus*) indicating the *prior* century of each maniple.

Other elements are also incorporated into the *signum*, either above or below the *phalerae* grouping. These include tablets inscribed with the unit's title, wreaths (probably denoting awards), fortress turrets (possibly commemorating the storming of a fortification), and emblems taken from the Zodiac, indicating the legion's birth month. As no more than six *phalerae* seem to be placed on each *signum* in the surviving sculptural evidence, it is possible that the number of discs may denote which number century in the cohort it belonged to (six centuries per cohort): this would obviously be useful to a commander directing troops on the battlefield. In any case, standards had a key function in indicating unit positions and transmitting orders through their movements.

By the 4th century AD the *draco* seems to have become the most popular Roman standard, in use with both cavalry and infantry organisations. Originally a 'barbarian' standard of Eastern origin, it outlived the Empire and can be seen in use at least as late as the battle of Hastings in 1066. Its construction seems to have involved an open-jawed beast-head mounted on a staff, with a tube of coloured cloth attached at the 'neck' in such a way that the air of movement passing through the metal head inflated and animated the 'tail'.

Each individual century in both legionary and auxiliary

Opposite: Roman standard reconstructions exhibited in the Römische-Germanische Zentral Museum, Mainz, and attributed to Dr. Ludwig Lindenschmidt, a 19th century pioneer in the authentic depiction of the Roman soldier based on archaeological evidence. Left to right: (1) *Aquila* of *Legio XIIII Gemina*, based on the grave *stele* of Gnaeus Musius at Mainz. (2) *Vexillum* depicting the winged goddess 'Victory', based on an original example found in Egypt and now in Russia. (3) Typical legionary cohort *signum* with *manus* in wreath, possibly denoting the prior century of a maniple. (4) Auxiliary infantry *signum* of the VII Raetian Cohort, recruited in what is now Switzerland.

Right: Grave *stele* of Gnaeus Musius, *aquilifer* of *Legio XIIII GMV*, from which the Lindenschmidt 'eagle' reconstruction is derived. This *stele* is extremely important for the *Legio XIIII* reconstruction group, as it also identifies the specific shield emblem which they have duplicated. Evidence strongly indicates that each legion (and probably auxiliary cohorts as well) had their own distinctive shield emblems, and this is one of the rare instances where an emblem can be identified to a particular legion.

Opposite: *Signifer* of *Legio XIIII Gemina Martia Victrix* based on the grave *stelae* of two standard bearers of this legion with nearly identical costume and standards. Below the *phalerae* both *stelae* show the Capricorn emblem as depicted in the reconstruction. Also on both *stelae*, a second human 'head' appears to be resting on the deceased's shoulder. This can be confidently interpreted as a full-face helmet, as usually associated with Roman 'cavalry sports' equipment. Reconstruction has shown that when not being worn the helmet can rest comfortably on the shoulder, held in place by the weight of the animal pelt. A bearskin was chosen for this reconstruction due to the large claws depicted on the *stele*, and the common depiction of bear pelts worn by *signifers* in Roman sculpture. The oval shield is based on both original *stelae*, but as they both show the inside of the shield the emblem on the Musius *stele* is depicted here.

Above: *Signifer* and *cornucen* of *Legio XXI Rapax* of Augustan date. The *signum* is of typical form, with an inscribed tablet below the spearpoint indicating 'Cohort I'; this is based on a surviving fragment from Bonn. The caped mail shoulder doubling as shown on the Faustus and Secundus *stelae* are clearly seen here. For comfort the face plate of the enclosed helmet has been removed and is carried tied to the belt. In addition to the two *stelae* already mentioned which depict the full-face helmet worn by *signifers*, a similar face plate dating to the period of the Teutoburg disaster (9 AD) was found near Osnabruck. It is unlikely that the cavalry brought 'sports equipment' on this campaign, indicating that these types of helmets had other purposes.

Right: Grave *stele* of Quintus Luccius Faustus, *signifer* of *Legio XIIII Gemina Martia Victrix* during the later 1st century AD. Surprisingly, a nearly identical *stele* of *signifer* Gaius Vaerius Secundus of the same legion also survives. The only appreciable difference betwen the two is that six *phalerae* are displayed by Faustus, and only three by Secundus. Clearly shown is the caped form of shoulder doubling on the mail shirt, more commonly associated with Roman cavalry. On both *stelae* the shield appears to be oval, as in the case of the legion's *aquilifer* G. Musius. Most reconstruction groups and artists today equip *signifers* and *aquilifers* with small round *parma* shields, based on their depiction on Trajan's Column.

A detachment of *Legio XIIII GMV* including a *signifer* (here wearing a variant costume including a bronze *lorica squamata*, and the breeches normally associated with auxiliary troops), a *centurio* and a *cornucen* trumpeter. They are drawn up at the east *via principia* gate of the Saalburg fort. Although originally designed to accomodate a single auxiliary cohort, in this photograph it could easily represent a legionary *castra* – a permanent base strategically sited behind the frontier defences – since these were essentially similar, though much larger.

As the barbarians generally lacked siege engines, Roman garrisons in the West had relatively unimpressive defences. Archaeology has shown that the walls of this fort, like so many other Roman buildings, would have been plastered smooth, with incised red-painted lines to simulate massive masonry block construction.

Right: A *signifer* of *Legio XX Valeria Victrix* dating from the mid- to late 1st century AD, carrying a typical *signum* as portrayed on Trajan's Column. It is possible that the hand indicates the *prior* (first) century of the maniple, and the spearpoint the *posterior*. The dagged scale shirt and bearskin pelt are also derived from Trajan's Column. This reconstruction includes a regular service helmet, here of 'Imperial Gallic' form, instead of the more ceremonial types of the previous reconstructions.

Opposite: *Vexillarius* of *Legio VI Victrix*, circa late 1st century AD. The bull would represent the Zodiac month of the legion's birthday, and although there is no concrete evidence that legionary flags were decorated in such a manner, there is some precedent in the documented display of zodiacal symbols on other forms of standard. A dagged mail shirt without shoulder doubling is typically seen on the various standard bearers depicted on Trajan's Column. The noticeable belly is not an indication of an unfit soldier! When a mail shirt is belted a 'bag' has to be left loose above the belt, or the movement of the shoulders and arms is restricted.

Below: The *vexillum* of *Legio XIIII Gemina Martia Victrix* being removed from its shrine in the fort's *principia*, where the legion's standards were kept when not on campaign. This reconstruction bears only the legion's name, as on both the *Legio II Augusta* sculptural examples. A departure is the addition of *Legio XIIII's* zodiacal emblem, the Capricorn surmounting the *vexillum*. Examples of this practice are depicted on Trajan's Column.

Right: A more elaborate *vexillum* also depicting the Taurus, this time executed in embroidery rather than paint, and belonging to *Legio X Gemina*. A more elaborate spearpoint is utilized in this reconstruction, of a type associated with a *beneficarius* – one of the soldiers who discharged special duties on the staff of senior officers. Carrying the unit *vexillum* could well have been among these duties.

Opposite: *Vexillum* of *Legio XX Valeria Victrix*. While the boar is not a symbol from the Zodiac panoply, there is some evidence that it was used as a symbol in this legion. This includes tile antefixes from Holt bearing a boar above the inscription *'LEG XX'*, and a bronze decoration in the French National Library which associates *Legio XX* with a boar, and *Legio II Augusta* with a Capricorn.

54

Opposite: *Imago* of auxiliary cohort attached to *Legio XX Valeria Victrix* based on the *stele* of Genialis, *imaginifer* of the VII Raetian Cohort from Mainz, Germany. The *imago* portrait depicted here is that of Vespasianus, which would date this reconstruction group to the period between 69 and 79 AD. Unlike the Genialis *stele*, the reconstructed *imaginifer* carries the *parma*, often associated with standard bearers on Trajan's Column and other monuments.

Left: Grave *stele* of Genialis. This and other *stelae* of auxiliary standard bearers seem to suggest that the face of the animal pelt has been removed, possibly to visually subordinate them to legionary standard bearers, the masks of whose pelts are invariably left intact.

Below: Both infantry and cavalry of the late Empire carried *draco* standards, gradually adopted after the defeat, and typical absorption into the Roman forces, of Sarmatian heavy armoured cavalry from the 2nd century onwards. This reconstruction is based on one recovered at Niederbeiber, a cohort fort on the German *limes*.

Below: Another standard bearer's *parma*, this one a reconstruction belonging to *Legio X Gemina*. The dimensions were ascertained from a fragment of a shield cover excavated at Castleford and dated between 70 and 80 AD. The scene depicts a Roman triumphal procession derived largely from the triumph of Titus after the Jewish War.

Right: The excavated shield cover fragment is of particular interest as the stitch pattern indicates decoration with leather or cloth appliqué. *Legio X* has reconstructed the cover using two contrasting shades of leather. A number of other 1st century AD leather fragments attributed to either shield faces or covers also exhibit decorative stitching, indicating that some shield designs could have been applied panels rather than simply painted. This might explain why on so many monuments Roman shield design was executed in relief, rather than merely painted.

ARTILLERY

Though the artillery engines used by the Romans were primarily Greek inventions, the Romans were the first army in the world to develop the fairly modern concept of assigning heavy weapons as part of the regular establishment of an infantry company (i.e. the legionary century) and to employ this artillery in the battle of manoeuvre. This is confirmed by the writings of Vegetius, who in the 4th century AD stated that each century of the 'old' legions (presumably meaning those of the 3rd century) possessed an arrow – shooting catapult, and each cohort a stone-throwing *ballista*. It is probable that this artillery allowance dates from much earlier, as in his description of the Roman army during the 1st century AD Jewish Revolt the historian Flavius Josephus mentions that the three legions besieging Jotapata had a total of 160 artillery pieces.

The Romans employed two types of projectile-throwing siege engines: *catapulta,* which were arrow-shooters; and *ballistae,* stone-throwers capable of projecting ammunition ranging from the size of oranges to 70lb boulders. The predominant artillery piece in the Roman army was the arrow-shooting *scorpio,* which could be mounted in a cart and employed on the battlefield as true field artillery. It was not unknown, however, to employ stone-throwers on an open battlefield, as was the case with the Vitellian forces in the battle of Cremona in 69 AD.

The light arrow-shooting catapult was markedly improved during the last quarter of the 1st century AD. The new model used an iron frame instead of wood, allowing the springs to be wider spread for increased power. Unlike its wooden predecessors, its largely metal composition also defied rain and humidity, and the springs were now encased in bronze tubes. This is the catapult depicted on Trajan's Column.

The *onager* (wild ass) is the best known of all ancient artillery, though it came into common use only towards the end of the Roman Empire. Known as early as 200 BC, it probably did not come into widespread use earlier due to its inferiority when compared to the twin-armed torsion machines. Its popularity in the later period probably lay in its being far easier to construct, and requiring a less skilled crew to maintain and operate than the more complicated dual-armed engines.

A number of ancient treatises on artillery have survived to this day, undoubtedly preserved due to their potential military value. Indeed, the artillery of the Greeks and Romans may well have been superior to that of medieval man before the invention of gunpowder. From these ancient plans and formulae attempts have been made to reconstruct ancient artillery over the past hundred years or so.

Above: A small *ballista* of *Legio XX Valeria Victrix,* manned here by members of its auxiliary contingent in Flavian period dress. This engine is based on the technical description of Vitruvius, an artillery expert of the late 1st century BC.

The most impressive of these efforts known to us are those of General E. Schramm of the Prussian army immediately prior to World War I. Schramm reconstructed a number of different ancient catapults, some of which were probably known to the ancients only in theory (such as a model whose torsion was provided by compressed air cylinders). Most of these catapults survive, and can be seen at the Saalburg Museum near Bad Homburg, Germany. (Unfortunately the larger examples were destroyed during World War II.)

Schramm tested the range of his reconstructions with impressive results. For example, his 'three-span' catapult (one firing an arrow of this length, approx. 27ins) had a range of 369.5 metres. The largest of his onager reconstructions threw a 1.8kg stone over 300 metres. (Both of these machines were destroyed in World War II.) In each case horsehair was used to form the torsion springs; greater distances would probably be achieved if animal sinew were incorporated. Many catapults today use torsion springs of modern materials such as nylon rope, and their performance is thus of little value to the historian.

The present director of the Saalburg, Dr. Dietwulf Baatz (a former artilleryman himself) has followed in Gen.Schramm's footsteps, continuing to research ancient artillery with the help of numerous new archaeological discoveries and the aid of the computer. 59

Above: Members of a *Legio XIIII* 'scorpion' crew steady the frame as one member prepares to tighten the springs with a torque wrench. This reconstruction is carefully based on the remains of a catapult lost in the battle of Cremona in 69 AD by *Legio IIII Macedonica,* and uses the correct bronze spring washers and horsehair skeins. This weapon is especially appropriate for the *Legio XIIII* group, as the inscription on the bronze front plate of the original dates the catapult to 45 AD, when *IIII Macedonica* was stationed in Mainz; *XIIII Gemina* was also in Mainz until summoned for the invasion of Britain in 43 AD. It is likely, then, that *Legio XIIII* catapults were constructed in the same Mainz workshop as those for *Legio IIII,* and would have been identical except for the inscription on the front plate.

Below: Original bronze front plate of *Legio IIII Macedonica* catapult recovered on the battlefield near Cremona where the succession of Vespasianus to the throne was secured in a bloody battle in October 69 AD. (It was originally thought to be a plate from a 'legionary pay chest', and the aperture through which the arrow was shot, the keyhole.) This plate, and surviving bronze spring washers – whose diameter is central to the calculation of the whole dimensions of a *scorpio* – were among the primary sources used in the *Legio XIIII* reconstruction.

Above: Gen. Schramm's 1916
reconstruction of the Greek
Ampurias catapult on the
ramparts of the Saalburg Roman
fort reconstruction. This model
of the 2nd Punic War era differs
little from the arrow-shooting
'scorpions' used until the later 1st
century AD when they were
superceded by the iron-framed
cheiroballista. This catapult was
still able to shoot an arrow 285
metres in 1979.

Right: An *onager* of *Legio XX Valeria Victrix* captured just at the moment of discharge. Though the *onager* would have been known in the Flavian period which this group depicts, it would not have been a common weapon due to its inferiority when compared to dual-armed *ballistae*. Much simpler to construct than a *ballista*, the *onager* may occasionally have been used during this period as easy-to-build supplementary artillery when additional siege firepower was required.

Below: *Legio XIIII* two-man catapult crew carrying their 'Cremona'-type arrow-shooter. Ancient artillery formulae classify this as a 'three-span' machine, indicating an arrow of this length (67cm). This is determined by the diameter of the original bronze washers, copied here as closely as possible.

The *Legio XIIII* 'scorpion' in position to provide covering fire for the legion, as it may have appeared on a British beach during the 43 AD invasion. Such a catapult would be served by a two-man crew, though an eight-man *contubernium* would be responsible for it. In this simulation the remaining contubernium members are detailed to provide security and to move the piece rapidly as the situation might require.

ON CAMPAIGN

O ne of the more significant rewards of Roman 'living history' efforts is what can be learned through experimental archaeology – that is, constructing military equipment as accurately as possible, and then experimenting with its use to test theories on how the Romans may have accomplished a particular activity. The Roman marching pack has intrigued historians and laymen alike, since it was preserved for the ages on the spiral relief of Trajan's Column.

Probably all the Roman reconstruction groups extant have experimented with the marching pack. *Legio XXI Rapax* undoubtedly acquired the most experience on their 1985 march from Verona to Augsburg. Faced with carrying the formidable Republican *scutum*, their solution was to develop a complicated baldric system which literally turned the shield into a 'backpack', suspending it high enough not to interfere with marching. This was clearly not the mode of carrying as depicted on Trajan's Column, although there the far more manageable rectangular Imperial *scutum* is carried.

On a recent ten-day march *Legio VI Victrix* experimented with the marching pack, and carried the *scutum* in a like manner to *XXI Rapax*. This had disastrous results, as instead of Augustan mail these legionaries wore Corbridge cuirasses, which effectively destroyed the leather inner surface of their *scuta*. Clearly the 'backpack method' was unsuccessful when wearing this type of armour.

Legio XIIII had been experimenting with long-distance marching in Roman kit since the early 1980s. The greatest distance they achieved in a four-day period was 160km (40 per day) as an official 'military' team at the International Four Day Marches at Nijmegen, Holland.

As the armour, *scuta* and weapons exceeded the 40lb requirement for military marchers, the 'pack' was not carried during this exercise. Although elaborate baldric systems similar to those used by *Legio VI* and *XXI* were used, they were unsatisfactory when wearing a laminated cuirass; so the *scutum* was carried by hand for the entire march, sometimes with the aid of a simple shoulder strap to take some of the weight. With the success of this march, the next step was to incorporate the march pack. It was found that if the pack was laid directly against the back of the shoulder the pole balanced the load, and did not have to be held at all, merely guided occasionally against the inside curve of the shield. At all times the shield was carried in the hand, as the shields appear to be on Trajan's Column. The only difference on the Column is that the packs are held well above the shoulder. It is likely that the artist did this for clarity, as otherwise the packs would be obscured by the soldiers' heads.

Some interesting conclusions can be drawn from these experiments. Firstly, the Republican *scutum* may well have been carried like a pack, with straps high on the back, the mail armour of the period not damaging the shield's interior. The biggest drawback of this system is that the soldier would be relatively helpless in a surprise attack, and easily knocked on his back like a turtle.

Secondly, the system of carrying the *scutum* in the left hand, *pila* in the right, and balancing the pack on the shoulder is clearly viable with the shorter Imperial *scutum*, and most resembles the shields' position as carried with the pack on Trajan's Column. Carrying the Republican *scutum* in this manner over extended periods, however, is extremely tiring and awkward, particularly for men under 5 ft 6ins in height.

Conclusion: the cut-down Republican *scutum* may have been a product of Marius' time when the legionary was first required to carry his complete fighting and subsistence equipment. True, the full-size Republican shield is still seen in sculpture afterwards; but it is clear that Roman armies did not at once adopt Marius' reforms, and that the Republican *scutum* served ceremonial functions long after it ceased to be used in the field.

Left: *Signifer* and *mulio* of *Legio XXI Rapax* on the march from Verona, Italy, to Augsburg, Germany in 1985. The mules carry two tents, mill stone, pallisade stakes and tools. The soldiers wear the heavy woollen hooded cloak called the *paenula*. The Roman army normally allocated one mule per each eight-man *contubernium* and one mule for the centurion, who had a private tent.

Roman marching camp pallisade being constructed by members of *Legio XXI Rapax*. The exact employment of the pallisade stake (*pilum muralis*) is not known: it may have been formed into a simple lashed fence as here, or tied crosswise along a horizontal beam to form chevaux-de-frise for gateways, etc. It is a versatile device, and was probably used in many different ways.

The ditch, spoil and turf rampart, and stake fence thrown up around the overnight camp by all units on the march on active service provided good protection against a surprise night attack, destroying the impact of an enemy rush before it could close with the defenders – here the Augustan legionaries of *Rapax* practise the technique behind a short demonstration section.

Above: A legionary of the Augustan-date *Legio XXI Rapax* adjusts the centre pole of his leather *papilio* (butterfly),as the Romans called their camp tents. Some writers have suggested that this name refers to the cocoon-shape of the tent when rolled; actually, when the tent is laid flat prior to rolling it looks very much like a butterfly, each half forming a convincing 'wing'. This tent is based on fragments found at Newstead, Scotland, and Valkenburg, Holland. It is made of calfskin, as are the Newstead fragments, and required 36 hides in its construction.

Right: The Roman *caliga*, or marching boot. These are based on well-preserved examples found at Mainz. If properly fitted this is an excellent form of footwear, and can last for hundreds of miles. They require daily maintenance, however, which primarily involves the replacement of hobnails before the sole becomes worn.

Below: The *scutum* was protected from the elements when off parade or out of battle by a leather cover; the plywood can double in weight if it becomes soaked with rain. Since the leather was probably oiled it may have been dark brown in colour. Fragmentary remains of original covers sometimes have pierced leather appliqué-work stitched on, showing unit designations and designs. Though there are, obviously, no surviving examples, *Legio XIIII* have experimented with speculative but plausible scraps of old red tunic cloth inserted between cloth and appliqué panel, giving contrast to what would otherwise be virtually invisible details of the pierced design. Although pure guesswork, this is believable, and unprovable one way or the other.

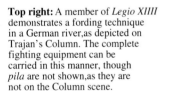

Top right: A member of *Legio XIIII* demonstrates a fording technique in a German river, as depicted on Trajan's Column. The complete fighting equipment can be carried in this manner, though *pila* are not shown, as they are not on the Column scene.

Above: The original Roman rectangular shield from Dura Europos, and surviving oval shields, have a horizontal grip, as shown on this *Legio XIIII* reconstruction. It has been suggested that this grip is unwieldly, and that a vertical handle would be more suitable in combat; but ten years of practical experiments have proved the contrary. The horizontal grip gives more stability when receiving blows, and allows comfortable carrying with the arm at full stretch, as demonstrated by this group on a four-day, 100-mile march.

Opposite and left: A legionary of *Legio XIIII* with his marching pack at the evening halt. The large linen sack contains his cloak and any spare clothing. The leather satchel holds such items as eating utensils, razor, tools, and personal effects. A netted bag (see detail view of kit below) holds ration grain, balanced on the pack by a bronze cooking pot and *patera* – skillet/mess tin. A metal water canteen can be seen slung behind the right shoulder in the close-up.

Below: The components of the march pack disassembled. The water bottle is based on several similar examples found in Britain and Germany; some are equipped with locks, indicating that they may have been intended for more than water! It is likely that less expensive containers such as pitch-lined leather flasks, animal bladders, gourds or net-covered ceramic vessels may have been more typical canteens. The leather satchel is based on an example from Hod Hill in Britain, which resembles those portrayed on Trajan's Column. There is some question whether this is actually a soldier's satchel, as the opening is barely wide enough to admit a hand. The string net bag holds an inner sack of linen which contains the soldier's grain issue. The clothing bag pictured here is linen also, though may have been of calf- or goatskin instead, which would provide better waterproofing.

Above: Members of a *Legio XIIII contubernium* in camp preparing a meal. Grain is ground to flour on the millstone, which on the march would be transported by the squad's mule. The ground meal could be boiled with water to form a porridge. Here the legionaries are forming 'loaves' which will be placed in the hot ashes of their camp fire for baking.

Right: *Legio XIIII* in camp, using their *pila* as spits to broil game birds foraged somewhere on the line of march. (The javelin shanks were untempered, so no serious damage would be done to them if used in this way.) The usual grain porridge and rough 'loaves' would be supplemented with meat and vegetables bought or bartered from camp followers, or hunted and gathered when opportunities allowed.

Opposite bottom: Camp of *Legio VI Victrix*. Like the *Legio XXI Rapax* and *XIIII GMV* reconstruction groups, *Legio VI Victrix* has complete marching equipment and has carried out long-distance marching experiments, the most recent a nine-day, l50km trek beginning here at Ladenburg, site of a Roman cohort fortress. On sunny days covers would probably be left off the shields to keep them as dry as possible. Note the variation in design distinguishing the centurion's shield (left) from those of his men. In this legion the *torquata* (wreathed) motif has replaced the familiar wings and thunderbolts usually seen on the legionary *scutum*, and can be found on Trajan's Column.

72

Left: Probable reconstruction of a type of legionary's tunic based on Trajan's Column. A wide neck opening allowed it to fall from one shoulder for freedom of movement during vigorous labour; it could be closed up by knotting at the back of the neck. This phenomenon is illustrated on the Column and in other contemporary sculpture.

Tunic colour is much debated. A red tunic can be seen beneath the armour of the 'guard' in the so-called Magistrate's Court scene at Pompeii, dating from the mid-1st century. A 2nd century Roman-type tunic found in a cave near Ein Gedi, Israel, retains this strong red shade; it was dyed with alizaran, obtained from the roots of the *rubia tintorium*, stated by Pliny to be the most important source of red dye for leather and woollens. White tunics are frequently found in Roman art, but almost without exception these are 'dress' garments worn without armour. White would be highly impractical for wear with mail or plate armour, or on campaign; red would hide rust and blood stains much better.

Overleaf: Camp of *Legio XIIII Gemina Martia Victrix*. This presents a good comparison of two different leather tent reconstructions. At left is one based on calfskin fragments from Newstead, as reconstructed by Sir Ian Richmond. The tent at right is based on very recent discoveries of a more complete goatskin tent section from Vindolanda on the English-Scottish border. The former is probably a typical *contubernium* tent and corresponds well with the depictions on Trajan's Column. The Vindolanda tent is probably that of a junior centurion, based on the contemporary description of a Roman camp by Hyginus. Hyginus allots l0 square feet (Roman) for the *contubernium* tent, but double that width for the centurion's.
Because of the high walls of the Vindolanda tent, if it were only about l0ft square (as the fragments seem to indicate) it would still require about 5ft on each side for the guylines – unlike the Newstead tent, which would need only about a foot for the guylines because of the very low side walls. Since the centurion's tent was essentially his 'office' the higher headroom does make sense. It is unlikely that a junior centurion's tent could have been much larger than 10 square feet as he had to carry it and his equipment on a single mule just as the legionaries did. The senior centurions (*primi ordines*) had larger 'wall tents', as did tribunes and other high-ranking officers, and probably had wagons to carry them in. Several styles of these tents are depicted on Trajan's Column.

A work detail return to a stone fortress, with a cavalry security escort. The soldiers carry typical Roman pioneer tools: an iron-shod wooden spade, a *dolabra* (pick) and a mattock. This double gate at the Saalburg is the main entrance through which the *via praetoria* leads to the administrative centre of the fort.

LEGIONARY CAVALRY

As in so many societies, service in the cavalry was the prerogative of the Roman upper class – those who could afford horses, probably already had them, and knew how to ride them. This is the origin of the term for the Roman nobility, the 'equestrian class'.

In the 'Servian' army of the 4th century BC the cavalry arm consisted of 18 'centuries', each numbering closer to 60 or 80 than the nominal 100 implied by the term. The 'post-Camillan' legion described by Polybius had about 300 integral cavalrymen, divided into ten *turmae* of around 30 men each; in turn, the *turmae* were divided into three ten-man sections, each led by a *decurio*.

By the time of Marius the legionary cavalry seem to have disappeared, possibly eliminated during his reforms. By the early Empire, however, they were back again, 120 strong, in four *turmae* of 30, as described by Flavius Josephus during the Jewish Revolt. This small force could hardly have been decisive in battle, and was most likely relegated to escort and messenger duties. The real cavalry branch of the army were the auxiliary *alae*, regiments numbering 500 or 1,000 men.

Vegetius states that the cavalry in the later legions numbered 22 *turmae*, making the force well over 600 strong. This dramatic increase is usually attributed to Septimius Severus or Gallienus (reigned c.253-268), both of whom did much to increase the proportion of cavalry in the army.

Experiments with reconstructions of Roman cavalry saddles and other equipment by author-illustrator Peter Connolly, and Dr. Marcus Junkelmann's *Ala II Flavia* (of which this writer is a member), are doing much to reappraise the role of Roman cavalry and its tactical abilities. Ignorant of the excellent Roman saddle, and aware only of its lack of stirrups, past historians have generally assigned the Roman cavalry less than its due importance. These modern experiments are proving that Roman cavalry could perform all the roles expected of the mounted arm without the use or need of the stirruped saddle.

As the scope of this book is largely limited to the Roman legionary, it is impossible adequately to discuss here the Roman cavalry and the exciting experimental archaeology activities of those who have recreated it. For this reason a companion volume devoted exclusively to the Roman cavalry is in preparation.

Above and opposite: Roman legionary cavalryman of the 2nd century BC Punic and Macedonian wars. The Attic helmet – a somewhat Latinized form of a Greek original – seems to have been popular, and its influence can be seen in evolved cavalry helmets of the Imperial period. Celtic influence can begin to be seen in cavalry equipment at this period: the mail shirt has typical cape-like shoulder doubling (and a slit at each side of the bottom edge, giving ease of movement when mounting and dismounting). The long sword, a slashing weapon with longer reach than the infantry *gladius,* is of Greek pattern, and may have remained the cavalry sidearm until the *spatha* was developed specifically for cavalry use. Note the large round wooden shield with a wooden spindle boss. The four-horned Celtic saddle does not appear in Republican sculpture and probably saw widespread Roman use only after Julius Caesar's Gallic conquests.

Right: Legionary cavalryman of the early Principate. The helmet, from an original found at Norwich, England, has simulated locks of hair chased into the iron skull. A characteristic feature of Imperial period cavalry helmets is the extension of the cheek guards to cover the ears, often shaped as simulated ears. The large shield gives good protection; it is based on well-preserved shield covers from Valkenburg, Holland (where important saddle fragments have also been found). The painted design is hypothetical; it represents the *Ala II Flavia* reconstruction group which has done so much for 'experimental archaeology' in the field of Roman cavalry.

Left: Dismounted 1st century AD
cavalryman, wearing Gallic-type
mail shirt and a helmet modelled
on a find at Koblenz-Bubenheim
in Germany; this resembles the
Norwich helmet, but differs in
having a thin bronze sheet
embossed with 'hair' applied
over a smooth iron skull. Note
the four horns of the saddle,
which give a secure seat even
without stirrups; and the
campaign equipment. Leather
saddle thongs secure a cloak and
blanket; a leather satchel and
bronze *patera* hang from one
horn, and a water bottle and
grain bag from the opposite side,
as does the leather-covered
shield. The small size of cavalry
mounts is attested by skeletal
finds at fort sites.

An officer of horse, early 5th century, reconstructed by John Harris of the *Milites Litoris Saxoni*: an amalgam of items which have no certain dates, this is a speculative but convincing reconstruction of a cavalry officer, probably of barbarian *foederati* mercenaries, fighting for Rome (or a Roman leader) in perhaps the time of Honorius, as the darkness finally fell over the Western Empire. The six-panel nasal *spangenhelm* is taken from a find in a later Vendel grave in Germany, but is very similar to several finds on late Roman sites, notably in Egypt. The heavily decorated tunic follows much contemporary evidence; the appliqué panels may have had rank or unit significance. The natural off-white of the wool cloak is a colour associated with officers; common soldiers have been shown in brown cloaks. The trousers are shown in several different dark colours; and the sturdy hobnailed leather shoes are one of many known designs. The *spatha* hangs from a typically Germanic metal-fitted waist belt; the staff is from the Piazza Armerina mosaic. The round shield is painted with the Christian *chi-rho* device flanked by a winged victory (or angel) presenting laurels to a portrait figure, perhaps the emperor? (Photographs John Eagle)

AUXILIARY INFANTRY

Even in the early Republic the Roman army had supplemented its strength with auxiliary troops. In the earlier times these were primarily specialist troops fulfilling roles in which Roman citizens – better utilized as legionary infantry – were unskilled. The best-known early auxiliaries were archers from Crete, and slingers from the Balearic Islands.

In addition to such specialist troops, by Imperial times there were cohorts of regular infantry, equipped and organized in Roman fashion. No doubt the vast new resources of manpower brought about by the Empire's territorial expansion afforded the opportunity to supplement the infantry branch with a new class of soldier. Auxiliary infantry, less valuable than citizen legionaries, performed the arduous duties of border surveillance and quelling minor incursions. This left the legions as consolidated, strategic reserves to be deployed only for real emergencies or major campaigns.

Perhaps over-emphasised in some texts, the supposedly 'lighter' equipment of *auxilia* versus legionaries suggests that auxiliary infantry served in a light infantry role. Some may well have done; but experiments with reconstructed equipment do not tend to bear this out completely. An authentically-replicated mail shirt ('typical' lst-2nd century body armour of the auxiliaries) is heavier than a legionary's laminated iron cuirass. The auxiliary's oval shield is only slightly lighter, its greater height compensating for the greater width of the legionary *scutum*.

It is possible that the differences in equipment were deliberate, so that the legionary was better armed and equipped to ensure success against the non-citizen auxiliaries in the event of revolts against Roman rule (which did happen on occasion). This may also explain why auxiliaries were never organized in units larger than 1,000-man cohorts (even this was rare, 500 being more common); and also why the auxiliaries were not equipped with the devastating offensive *pilum*. As for auxiliary infantry employment as scouts and flank guards, this may only have been because they were more expendable, and their loss less important in the ambushes and encounter skirmishes inseperable from these kinds of duties.

Auxiliary troops were generally non-citizens from the conquered provinces, who after 25 years' service in the army would receive the coveted Roman citizenship. Their sons would then have the right to enlist in the legions. In this way, the ethnic make-up of the legions changed from essentially 'Italian' to a diversity probably not unlike that seen in the racial make-up of the modern reconstruction groups seen in these pages.

Above: An auxiliary archer, probably recruited from an Eastern province as suggested by his conical helmet. His composition bow is one of several types known to have been in use. This one is made of wooden layers backed by animal sinew; a more complicated version was made from glued sections of animal horn.

Opposite: Mid-1st century AD auxiliary infantry who form a detachment as part of the Ermine Street Guard (*Legio XX*) in England. This view illustrates a typical auxiliary shield design based on one portrayed on Trajan's Column, as well as the inside, showing the handgrip and wood strip reinforcements. Note the simple *hasta* (spear).

Above & right: Detail of the Auxiliary Infantry 'B' helmet worn by a member of *Cohors IIII Vindelicorum*, a German group representing auxiliaries who frequently conduct displays with *Legio XIIII*. The original on which this bronze replica is based was found in the Rhine at Mainz, like so many other helmets depicted in this book. Its simple design and lack of crest mounts are the reasons this helmet has been classified as auxiliary rather than legionary equipment.

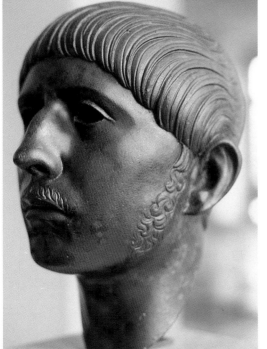

Top left: Rear view of an auxiliary, showing the method of carrying the shield, and the dagged-edge mail shirt and short breeches portrayed in sculptural sources, notably Trajan's Column.

Left: For those who think that long sideburns and moustaches among re-enactors of the Roman army are unauthentic, this photograph of an original 1st century AD Roman portrait bust is included... Modern facial hairstyles are, of course, discouraged in most groups, who would rather portray the typical than the unusual.

Above and opposite: An auxiliary infantryman of the early 2nd century AD, so dated by his Auxiliary Infantry 'C' helmet, similar to those depicted on Trajan's Column. This lone auxiliary is part of *Legio VI Victrix's* group, to show the various troop types in the Roman army besides the legionaries which the group depicts. With the introduction of crossed metal reinforces in the early 1st century AD, legionary helmets also lacked any visible means to affix a crest; but this helmet is believed to have belonged to an auxiliary due to its simple construction and bronze material. Most legionary helmets of this date are generally considered to have been made of iron. Bronze is a more expensive metal, but cheaper to work into a helmet; some examples were 'spun' on a lathe from annealed bronze sheet.

ROMAN RECONSTRUCTION GROUPS

For several years the only organised group which attempted to depict the Roman army in an authentic manner was the Ermine Street Guard in Great Britain. But no one group, of course, could hold a complete monopoly in such an interesting field, continuously made ever more popular as new archaeological finds and literature appear on the subject. Now, almost 20 years since 'the Guard' was first organised, there exist a number of other serious reconstruction groups which strive for accuracy.

It had been our intent to include in this book all of the known Roman military reconstruction groups which both maintain high standards of authenticity and have enough members to realistically qualify as viable units. Smaller, lesser known groups were also sought out for possible inclusion, though these either declined to respond or were not altogether ready for public scrutiny or comparison with the featured groups.

There are few if any time periods in which the accurate reconstruction of the uniform and equipment of the 'typical' soldier present a greater challenge than that of the Roman legionary. It is for this reason, of course, that Roman reconstruction groups are by no means common, and enjoy a somewhat elite status in the re-enactment world at large. Perhaps more than for any other replicated time period, there are more real 'craftsmen' in the ranks, attracted by the challenge of accurately reconstructing this fascinating equipment; and among those groups which promote 'living history' and experimental archaeology there is also the challenge of marching, drilling and even fighting in this equipment.

For purposes of acknowledging the various groups responsible for the photos and reconstructions seen in this book the author has quoted the title of the Roman 'unit' they normally represent, this being more appropriate than giving a modern society or club name.

Opposite: The oldest and best known of the Roman reconstruction groups is the Ermine Street Guard of Great Britain. Formed in 1972, the group depicts both legionary and auxiliary soldiers of the Roman army in Britain during the last half of the 1st century AD, with the most emphasis on the Flavian period. Though best known for their depiction of *Legio XX Valeria Victrix*, they carry here the *vexillum* of *Legio II Augusta* for a local display in an area where *Legio II* was once garrisoned. The Guard's great longevity has created challenges few of the newer groups have had to face. In their formative years less was known about Roman military equipment, and some reconstructions then thought to be authentic have more recently been rendered obsolete – to the chagrin of the members who have had to re-make them, and who deserve credit for this devotion to expensive and time-consuming accuracy. The unit's primary focus is the accurate reconstruction of Roman military equipment and the performance of educational public displays. The Ermine Street Guard publishes the journal 'Exercitus', which in addition to society news contains interesting articles relating to the Roman army, some by well known authors and archaeologists. Though vacancies may be limited in the uniformed display group itself, associate members are always welcomed and 'the Guard' can be reached at : Oakland Farm, Dog Lane, Crickley Hill, Witcombe, Gloucestershire, England.

Above: *Legio XIIII Gemina Martia Victrix* was organised in 1982 by the staff of a US Army museum in Frankfurt, Germany, and consists today of roughly equal numbers of Germans and Americans. The group primarily represents the named legion exactly 1,900 years earlier when it was stationed in nearby Mainz, and participated in the Chatti War in the surrounding Taunus Mountains, ca. 83 AD. No other reconstruction group has gone to such detail in its attempt to depict an actual Roman unit, as the shield emblem, *signum*, *signifer* and *aquila* are all based on original *Legio XIIII* examples. Moreover, the bulk of its armour and weapon reconstructions are based on original artifacts from the Mainz area dated to the *Legio XIIII* occupation period. In addition to reconstruction work and public displays *Legio XIIII* conducts intensive 'practical archaeology' experiments such as making arduous, long-distance marches, practising various combat skills, and assembling a complete 'living history' camp in which members can maintain a '24 hour a day' Roman impression during both public displays and private wilderness 'manoeuvres' in army training areas. As the group is now well enough established, opening it to wider membership and the production of a journal are under way; but unfortunately history has a habit of repeating itself. . . .

In 92 AD *Legio XIIII GMV* was transferred from Mainz to Carnuntum in Pannonia. Incredibly, exactly 1,900 years later, with the reduction of US forces in Europe, the present *Legio XIIII* 'headquarters' will depart the Mainz-Frankfurt area in 1992 for provinces yet unknown! Nevertheless a current contact address for the group is Dan Peterson, Director, 3d Armored Division Museum, Headquarters, 3d Armored Division, APO NY 09039.

91

Previous page: *Legio XXI Rapax* was 're-activated' in Germany shortly after *Legio XIIII*, though the two groups were unaware of each other's existence until they were both invited to the 2000th Anniversary of the founding of Augsburg in 1985. *Legio XXI* entered the city far more spectacularly than *Legio XIIII*, having marched over the Alps from Verona, Italy in the complete equipment of Augustan-date Roman legionaries. Led by the Bavarian military historian Dr. Marcus Junkelmann, their 23-day Alpine march – eating, sleeping, and marching entirely in Roman persona – must rank as one of the most signicant re-enactment events, of any time period, yet undertaken by a reconstructed military unit. This 'atmospheric' photo was snatched during the march. *Legio XXI* existed primarily for this experiment in practical archaeology, which was partly the subject of an excellent book by Dr. Junkelmann entitled 'Die Legionen des Augustus' ('The Legions of Augustus'), which unfortunately for English readers is only available in a German language edition (Verlag Philipp von Zabern, Mainz).

After the experiment *Legio XXI* was essentially de-activated, much of its equipment being scattered to museums and private collections. Occasionally there are reunions, such as a recent display at Augsburg where they again marched with *Legio XIIII*; and a new Roman group, again founded by Dr. Junkelmann, is described at the end of this chapter.

Right: *Legio VI Victrix* from Opladen, Germany is an excellent example of how dedication and hard work can effect an amazing transformation. When first contacted this group, then known only as the Opladen Roman Cohort, was a major Rhineland 'carnival' club. Impressive in its own right, with a *legatus*, six *tribunes*, a *centurio* and over 20 aluminium-armoured legionaries, the group also had all the attendant 'Hollywood' tents and camp equipage that would be the envy of any Italian 'sword and sandal' film producer. After inviting members of *Legiones XIIII* and *X Gemina* (see below) to their annual Roman festivals, where the groups shared knowledge and equipment sources, the Opladeners became determined to create an authentic unit of their own. Improvements seemed to come slowly; but then, after six months in the Persian Gulf, the author returned to find them transformed into a very respectable, though somewhat smaller unit, with complete marching equipment and a leather tent planned for next season.

Gemina Project, a new Roman group being formed in the Netherlands, recreates the *Legio X Gemina*, which is mentioned above and whose reconstructions are also displayed in this book. They felt that they were not quite ready to provide a unit photo, though by the time of publication should field a complete *contubernium* in the same very popular late 1st century AD gear as depicted by *Legiones VI*, *XIIII*, and *XX*. *Legio X* already produces a newsletter, and can be contacted at: Gemina Project, Pharus 309, 1503 Zandam, The Netherlands.

Two small but high-quality groups are based at Sittingbourne, Kent, England, and can both be contacted through: John Harris, 82 London Rd., Faversham, Kent ME13 8TA. The *Milites Litoris Saxoni* (Troops of the Saxon Shore) reconstruct the appearance of garrison troops in the 4th-5th centuries AD – representative photographs are published elsewhere in this book; and are co-located with a secondary unit reconstructing 1st century AD legionaries, temporarily titled *Legio IX Hispana*.

Above: As the subject of this book is Roman legionaries, the only reconstruction group dedicated entirely to Roman cavalry could not play a great part. It would be remiss, however, not to mention in closing this unique and extremely authentic reconstruction group. *Ala Secunda Flavia* was formed by the same Dr. Junkelmann who created *Legio XXI Rapax*, commencing as soon as the dust had settled from the Augsburg event. Like the legionaries of *XXI Rapax*, the cavalrymen of *Ala II Flavia* have trained, worked, slept and even eaten for weeks at a time in Roman fashion in some very impressive feats of 'living history'. Thus far the *Ala* has navigated most of the *limes* (Roman Imperial border) in Western Europe, and has conducted training camps in Italy which culminated in a race in the Circus of Maxentius, and a parade and ceremony in the Forum of Rome!

The group has made important breakthroughs in the reconstruction of the Roman saddle and other items of equipment, as well as experimentation in fighting tactics; the combined results may help rewrite what was previously believed about this often underrated, though nevertheless extremely important branch of the Roman army. Nearly all of the Roman cavalry, and over half of the infantry were auxiliaries. It is hoped that the story of *Ala II Flavia's* adventures in experimental archaeology, as well as a study of other reconstruction groups which depict 'the other half' of the Roman army, will be featured in a future sequel to this present volume.